D0499943

The
Happiness
Code

The Happiness Code

Ten keys to being the best you can be

Domonique Bertolucci

Published in 2012 by Hardie Grant Books

Hardie Grant Books (Australia)
Ground and Level One
Building One
658 Church Street
Richmond, 3121
www.hardiegrant.com.au

Hardie Grant Books (UK)
Dudley House, North Suite
34–35 Southampton Street
London WC2E 7HF
www.hardiegrant.co.uk

National Library of Australia Cataloguing-in-Publication Data:
Author: Bertolucci, Domonique.
Title: The happiness code : ten keys to being the best you can be /
             Domonique Bertolucci.
ISBN: 9781742702483 (hbk.)
Subjects: Happiness.
             Self-actualization (Psychology).
             Conduct of life.
Dewey Number: 158.1

Cover design, text design and typesetting by Raylee Sloane, Kinart
Typeset in Minion Pro 11.2/16pt
Permission to use quote by Mary Schmich courtesy of the Chicago Tribune
Printed and bound in China by C&C Offset Printing

For my darling Sophia

The most important thing is to enjoy your life
—to be happy—
it's all that matters.

AUDREY HEPBURN

Contents

Preface   xi

Introducing the Ten Keys   1

The First Key: Take Charge   7

The Second Key: Let It Go   27

The Third Key: Live for Now   47

The Fourth Key: Expect the Best   67

The Fifth Key: Back Yourself   89

The Sixth Key: Get Out of the Way   109

The Seventh Key: Be Grateful   129

The Eighth Key: Give All You Can   149

The Ninth Key: Keep It Up   169

The Tenth Key: Be Brave   189

Unlocking the Code   209

Acknowledgements   211

About the Author   213

Preface

Have you ever wondered why some people seem really, genuinely happy and yet others experience a near constant state of stress, frustration or disappointment? Why does happiness come so easily to some people? And how can you make sure it comes easily to you?

Happiness begins with a choice.

So many people are *waiting* to feel happy. They think they will be happy when they've done this or achieved that. But the truth is, enduring happiness is not a result of the things you've done, but the person you've chosen to be.

Somewhere in my mid-twenties, I made the decision to be happy. It's not that I was miserable before this time. If you asked most people who knew me, I'm sure they would have described me as a happy person. But as I've since learned, there is a big difference between being happy about things *as they are* and being happy *with who you are.*

The realisation that I had to change the way I created and sustained happiness came as the result of a really challenging and difficult time in my life. While I now look back on the whole period and lightheartedly call it my quarter-life crisis, the truth is I was working for a bully in a job I hated, ending a relationship I never should have started and deeply angry with myself for not being in possession of the perfect life I had been so sure would have been mine by now.

I cried a lot. My eyes were so puffy that I worried my face would change shape, forever! I remember thinking, 'I'm sure there is a great *learning experience* hidden in all this pain and heartache, but please … can I just hurry up and learn it?'

Finally, through my tears came some very real revelations about happiness: how I had sourced it in my life up until this point and what would have to change if my happiness was to be guaranteed in the future.

I learned I had to give up trying to achieve perfection; it was never going to happen. I stopped worrying about what other people might be thinking or saying about me and accepted that while some people liked me, others might not, and I learned to be okay with that. I stopped feeling guilty, full stop.

I discovered that I didn't have to stress if things weren't going my way or feel anxious about my future. Some things were within my control and others weren't, but as long as I believed in myself and in my potential, life would probably turn out just fine.

I let go of the expectations I held of the people around me; they no longer angered or frustrated me, nor did they have the power to hurt me. I learned that it was no more my place to judge them than it was theirs to judge me.

I found the courage to pursue my dreams and the commitment to see them through, but I realised that even if I had goals for the future, I could still enjoy each day for what it was, appreciating all the good that was already in my life.

Most of all, I remembered something my mother had been telling me since I was a little girl … that as long as I was giving my best, my best would always be good enough.

Introducing the Ten Keys

As a success coach, I have had the chance to examine the thoughts and feelings of hundreds of people. I have found that many people are so focused on changing themselves that they lose themselves in the process. Although their initial desire may have been for self-improvement, too often they use their new education and discoveries as fresh material with which to engage in critical, perfectionist behaviour, leading to frustration and anxiety, an erosion of self-belief, and ultimately a lack of enjoyment and fulfilment from everyday life.

When I share this observation, all too often the response I receive is, 'I'm just trying to be the best that I can be'. But what does being the *best you can be* really mean?

At last there is an answer.

The secret to experiencing lifelong happiness and contentment lies within these guiding principles— the Ten Keys.

Following is an outline of the Ten Keys; each chapter of this book represents a different key and explains the role it plays in creating lasting happiness and fulfilment.

The First Key: Take Charge
The Principle of Choice

The first and most important step in becoming the *best you can be* is to simply decide to be that person. Of course, that's much easier said than done. Most people find plenty of excuses to avoid being honest with themselves about who they are and what they really want from life. Make the choice to own up to your true potential and step into your brilliance.

The Second Key: Let It Go
The Principle of Acceptance

Don't waste energy trying to change or control things that are well beyond your control. Instead, focus on the things that are within your influence and find a peaceful acceptance of the rest.

The Third Key: Live for Now
The Principle of Presence

Don't live in the past, blaming your current reality on experiences from childhood, early adulthood or even last week. At the same time, don't be so busy dreaming of your future that you overlook or waste the opportunities that are presented to you today. It's important to accept the past, dream of the future, but live in the moment!

The Fourth Key: Expect the Best
The Principle of Optimism

If you expect things to turn out well, they usually do. Likewise, if you expect to be disappointed or let down, or to experience failure, then it's highly likely that will be your experience. Being optimistic is not about being naive or ignorant about potentially negative outcomes. Optimism is about expectation; expect the best from life and you will usually get it.

The Fifth Key: Back Yourself
The Principle of Belief

One of the most important ingredients in creating any success in life is to believe in it. You need to learn to believe in your dreams, your ideas and yourself. Other people will always try to lead you away from your dreams, not because they don't want you to be happy, but because they are governed by their own fear, self-doubt and limiting beliefs. When you truly believe, it's amazing what becomes possible.

The Sixth Key: Get Out of the Way
The Principle of Permission

So many people don't take ownership of the possibilities in their lives. They constantly blame other people, other times and other situations for their circumstances. The only person who can really hold you back in life is you. Overcome your limiting beliefs, ideas and attitudes and give yourself permission to truly shine.

The Seventh Key: Be Grateful
The Principle of Abundance

Very few people genuinely don't have enough money to get by, and yet so many affluent, healthy people constantly talk about all the things that they don't have. A poverty mentality is a serious affliction. When you focus on how much you already have, your true desires will be easily met and you will discover how little you genuinely need.

The Eighth Key: Give All You Can
The Principle of Generosity

Be generous, not just with the gifts you give, but also with how you give of yourself. To be truly generous you need to give your time, energy and spirit. Avoid judgement and be generous in your assessment of others. What you give in life will determine what you receive.

The Ninth Key: Keep It Up
The Principle of Commitment

It won't always be easy to do, be or have everything you want in life, but if your desires are genuine, over time these things will begin to come to you *with ease*. Don't give up or choose a more complacent path. If you are committed to being the best you can be, then you're already becoming that person.

The Tenth Key: Be Brave
The Principle of Courage

If you want to be the *best you can be*, you need to do the right thing, not the easy thing. I don't mean right or wrong in a black or white, moralistic sense; the principle of courage is about doing the right thing for you and having the courage to do it, even if at the time it feels like the hardest thing in the world!

When you apply these guiding principles to your life, you can feel confident you *are being* the best you can be and lifelong happiness and contentment will be yours.

If you would like to learn more about applying the Ten Keys and unlocking the secret to lifelong happiness and contentment in your life, you can download *The Happiness Code Workbook*, full of exercises, ideas and inspiration, free from **domoniquebertolucci.com**.

Take Charge
The Principle of Choice

Happiness begins with a choice.

If you want to be the best you can be, the kind of person who has lasting happiness and fulfilment in their life, you need to *choose* to be that person. Being happy doesn't have to be complicated. The minute you make the decision to be happy, you instantly become happier. Your perspective shifts and you start to see your world from the vantage point of someone who *is happy*. Of course, choosing to be happy isn't the only thing that you need to do, but unless you make the conscious decision to be happy, your other efforts could be wasted.

Being happy isn't something that you become 'one day', or something that you get when you cross off enough things on your life's to-do list. You don't decide, 'Being the best I can be, hmm … I think I'll give that a try next Tuesday'. True happiness is a way of life.

Happiness is a choice.
Choose to be happy
and you will be.

Think about the person you are right now. Are you someone who is happy, who takes life's ups and downs in your stride and brings a sunny, positive attitude to all that you do? Do you fundamentally believe that your life will be a good one and trust that good things will continue to happen for you?

Do you expect the best from yourself, stand up for what you believe in and maintain confidence in your right to the best life you can possibly live? Or have you chosen to be a different person altogether, personalising your negative experiences, and seeing them as things that are happening to *you*, rather than accepting that sometimes these things just happen?

Being the best you can be is not the same as trying to be perfect. The quest for perfection is a lost cause. It is entirely subjective and completely unachievable, so stop trying to be perfect. Stop trying to have the perfect body, the perfect hair or the perfect home. Stop trying to be the perfect partner, perfect friend, perfect parent, perfect homemaker or perfect provider. Say 'no' to trying to be the perfect boss, delivering the perfect report or being the perfect employee. And stop trying to perfect all of these things all at once!

If nothing you do is ever good enough, you will exist in a constant state of dissatisfaction, frustration and disappointment … with yourself. Not a great idea if your aim is to be happy! Releasing yourself from the burden of perfectionism is one of the most liberating things you can do but it doesn't mean slacking off, accepting average or becoming complacent in your life. It is about establishing what your best is and committing to that.

We can't all be amazing at everything. No matter how multi-talented you are there are simply not enough hours in the day to find the time to excel at everything. Choose your starring moments wisely and accept that at other things you may be just a little more ordinary. I know I am a brilliant parent, loving partner and loyal friend. And I accept that my best is a lot more average when it comes to my personal administration, preparing mid-week meals and sticking to my fitness routine.

Perfectionism is a lost cause.
Focus your energy on being
the best you can be.

Happiness is a state of being, not a state of having. It isn't something you get when you tick off items on a list: a new job, a new car, a new house or new shoes. While all of these things, and many others, may give you pleasure in the moment, they don't have an impact on your ability to sustain long-term happiness in your life.

*True happiness is a state of being,
not one of doing or having.*

When you focus on being the best you can be, you will experience a sense of calm in your life. There will still be days that are big-hitters, but more often than not you will enjoy a quiet sense of comfort, knowing that you gave your best and your best was good enough. Even on the days that aren't so great, as long as you gave your best, in that moment, at that time and under those circumstances, you will still be content.

Part of being truly happy is living the life you want to live. This isn't something that just happens by accident; at least, that is not the case for most people. Think about what your ideal life looks like: what you do, where you live, how you spend your time and who you spend it with. Rather than viewing these things as simply the circumstances of your life, things that just happen, consider the design of your life as a critical contributor to the happiness in your life. Not because you have all that you want, but because you will be actively creating the life that you want.

Even if you don't feel confident that you know what you want, don't allow that to become your excuse for being complacent about your life. It's true, many people don't feel clear about what they want from life, but most people are pretty sure about what they don't want. If you don't know what you want, use your knowledge of what you don't want as your starting point. Don't want to work in an office? Great, start exploring opportunities that would allow you to work outside the office. Don't want to live in the city? Start exploring a sea- or tree-change. Not happy about the job that you have? Start thinking about other things that you might like to do.

Oprah Winfrey said, 'If you want your life to be more rewarding you need to change the way you think'. If you are not experiencing all the happiness you deserve, think carefully about what changes you need to make and how you could be redesigning your life, so it becomes one you feel much better about living.

This concept of 'life design' can feel a little overwhelming at first, but don't pressure yourself into trying to create a perfect life in an instant. Start by looking at some quick wins or simple changes you could make. If you don't feel like you see your friends or family enough, invite them over. If you feel like you're stuck in a dead-end job, update your CV, or if you feel like your life would be more meaningful with a partner, join a dating site or service. The most important thing you can do is to consciously make choices that take you closer to the life you really want.

You only have one life. Make sure that yours is one you are happy to be living.

The good thing about starting small is that it builds your confidence and gets you used to the feeling of being in charge.

William was feeling really down. He was in a job he didn't particularly like, spending time with people he didn't particularly care for and drinking far more than he should. He was starting to worry that he was on a fast train to nowhere and his wife was fed up with him moaning about his life.

William couldn't remember the last time he felt really content, but he had a funny feeling he hadn't felt that way since he left university. Of course there were elements of his life that he was very happy with, like his marriage, but his overall feeling was one of discontent.

I wanted to examine the choices William had made since leaving university, but the problem was, he hadn't really been making choices. Rather than being a proactive participant, William had been letting his life happen to him. He had accepted a job doing something he was good at, but he had never stopped to ask himself if this was what he wanted to do. He was still hanging out with his high-school friends, without ever having asked himself if these were people who shared his values, goals or ideals. He was trying to inject some fun into his life by going out all the time, but all that was doing was giving him a different type of headache than the one he already had.

Feeling strong and empowered is a fundamental contributor to long-term, sustained happiness, but it is hard to feel that way if you don't take responsibility for your life and consciously make choices that support you in living the life you really want.

Although William realised he couldn't turn his life around in an instant, he now knew exactly what kind of life he wanted to create and he knew it was up to him to create it. He felt fully empowered and infinitely happier in his life.

One of the best things you can do if you want to create lasting happiness in your life is to get really clear about your values. So often, life can 'look good on paper', but if the life you are living is not in alignment with your values, you may find yourself feeling hollow and unfulfilled. Put simply, your values are the aspects of your life that are of most importance to you. Although just a series of words, your values provide a powerful insight into who you are and what matters most to you in life.

Having a clear understanding of your values makes it easier to set goals and create a fulfilling future. When you are faced with a decision, consider your values and look at the compromises each option requires. Consciously make choices that lead you towards a life that is fully aligned with all of your values, all of the time.

Focus on what matters.
Honour your values
and make decisions
that are aligned with them.

If you want to be truly happy in life, you need to ensure that the choices you make directly support your values. If they don't, you can be left feeling annoyed, angry or lost, no matter how good things might look from the outside.

Every choice or decision you make will have consequences. So often I speak with people who are feeling frustrated, dissatisfied and unhappy in their lives, but when I listen to them I can hear quite clearly that they are ignoring, rebelling against or resenting the consequences of the choices they have made.

Perhaps you have chosen to move to a larger house, but now feel frustrated because your social life is constrained by your mortgage payments. Maybe you have decided to work part time while your children are young, only to find that you feel resentful that your career is not as dynamic or progressing as rapidly as it once was.

It's important to recognise that every single decision has consequences and there is no point expending your energy raging against them. They are what they are. You don't have to like it, but you need to learn to accept the impact your choices will have on your whole life, not just the specific thing they relate to. If you are not willing to accept the effect your choice has, then you need to re-examine your options and see if there are other alternatives you feel more comfortable with.

When you make a choice, acknowledge all the consequences. That way you won't be left feeling compromised.

If you find that you don't want to choose a different option, then you need to accept your circumstances and find a way to say, 'My life might not be perfect, but it is the best it can be right now, and I am okay with that'. Remember that most stages of life won't last forever and if you are feeling constrained in a certain aspect of your life, you are likely to be liberated from this at some point down the track. Your children may leave home, giving you lots of spare time and energy; the boss that you really can't stand will eventually move on; and your mortgage will be paid off, housing prices will rise and you will find yourself significantly wealthier than you are right now.

Angela was faced with a career dilemma. She had chosen to accept a role in a dynamic technology start-up. She wanted to learn as much as she could because she knew it would really expand her options for the future.

Unfortunately for Angela, one of the downsides of this fast-paced organisation was that several people she worked with had been promoted more rapidly than they might have been in more traditional environments. Her boss was a classic case of having been 'promoted to his level of incompetence'.

Angela felt frustrated and trapped working in an environment where she found it difficult to have professional respect for the person she worked for, as well as several of the people she worked with.

Angela and I began to explore her choices and their potential consequences. She knew she had several options. She could resign at any point and go back to her old corporate life, look for a job in another start-up company, or stay where she was and accept that the consequences of this choice would include both excellent career development *and* a frustrating manager and colleagues.

Angela could see that with twelve months' experience in this job, a lot of new doors would open up for her. She decided to stay where she was for the duration and to accept that it was unlikely that she would be impressed or inspired by her boss during this time. By consciously accepting the consequences of her decision, she was able to dramatically reduce the level of stress and frustration that she had been feeling and return to feeling strong and empowered in her life.

There's no such thing as 'I have no choice'. Unless you are being held at gunpoint, there is always another choice you could be making. Circumstances may sometimes make it difficult for you to see all of your available options: you might be tired and exhausted by the demands of small children, experiencing significant financial stress or reeling from the shock discovery of a betrayal. Whatever your circumstances there will always be other options; you just need to choose to look for them.

There is no such thing as 'no choice'. There are always other options. Explore yours.

It may take time, energy or courage. Sometimes this may mean having to make the tough choice; other times the simple fact that you recognise you have options can be enough to make you feel more comfortable with the choice you have already made. Even if you don't feel directly responsible for the situation you find yourself in, you *are* responsible for how you manage this situation and, more importantly, how you turn it around.

Sometimes it can feel easier to stay where you are in life, to blame a lack of choice rather than to challenge the status quo and explore other alternatives. Many people feel secretly comfortable stuck at a dead end, and stepping outside of your comfort zone can be quite overwhelming. If you find yourself feeling this way, remind yourself that it's *your* life; you don't have to change it if you don't want to. But if you do decide to leave things as they are, then you must choose to accept your current situation. If you can say, 'I've explored the other options and I am going to accept this situation', your sense of contentment will increase.

When you find yourself in a situation where you feel like you don't have any choice, remind yourself that there is always another path you could be taking. It might not be the one you want to take and you might choose not to take it, but there are always other options worth exploring. The lateral thinking guru Edward de Bono tells us to begin with the most unlikely option and work from there; so often the exploration of the improbable leads to the discovery of exactly the right choice you need to make.

In every life, there will be good days and bad days, successes and failures, happy events, sad ones, triumphs and very occasionally tragedy … that's just the way it is. Unless you want to live like a hermit, there is no avoiding the *experience* of life. But when you understand how to sustain your own happiness, your happiness will be lasting and impervious to the ups and downs of your life.

While life's experiences can inspire great happiness or sadness in the moment, true happiness is not defined by what is going on today, this week or even this year. Real happiness is a state of *being* that comes from deep within.

Realising that you get to choose *how* you experience these events can be a life-changing discovery. Most people have a similar range of experiences over a lifetime, but it is how they choose to process these experiences that determines the level of happiness in their life. I am always inspired when I hear of people who have suffered extreme illness, loss or tragedy, only to rise above it in their determination to continue to live a full and meaningful life. I think it's such a dreadful waste when people choose to wallow in their misery, adopt a victim persona and act like they are the only ones ever to feel let down by life.

Don't be the victim in your life. Self-pity will never lead to happiness.

A full and interesting life will have its share of negative events and experiences. Do your very best to take these events and experiences in your stride. You don't have to deny your feelings or smother your emotions but you don't have to let them consume you either.

Self-pity never leads to happiness. Remind yourself that the situation may not be ideal, but it's rarely the worst that could ever happen.

Consciously or subconsciously, people don't always make the best choices for their long-term happiness. Look at the choices you are making in your life and if they are not genuinely working for you, ask yourself, 'What is the choice I am *really* making here?'

If you are in a relationship where you are not fully respected, ask yourself, 'What choice am I really making by continuing to be involved in this relationship?' You might tell yourself that you are choosing to be modern and liberated or are blinded by love, but the choice you're really making might be to perpetuate your low self-esteem by reinforcing the message that you don't really deserve someone's love.

If you find that you drink an unhealthy amount, you might tell yourself that you are choosing to relax and unwind with a few drinks after work and you just got caught up in the moment, but maybe the real choice you have made is to deny your alcoholic tendencies or to shorten your life expectancy.

Don't sabotage your chance for happiness. Own up to the real choices you are making.

You might choose to stay in a job you hate, spend all the money you earn and then some, and tell yourself that you deserve to cheer yourself up, but the real choice you've made could be that you are trapping yourself in your job by getting yourself into debt and needing your income to repay that debt.

Examine every aspect of your life and ask yourself, 'What am I really choosing here, and can I really expect that choice to bring me lasting happiness?' You might be surprised what you uncover.

You don't have to choose to be happy. You can continue with your life just the way it is. But why not give it a try? The simple shift in perspective from making this choice can have the most profound impact on your life.

One of my favourite thoughts about happiness comes from the original *Domestic Goddess*, Nigella Lawson. Although Nigella lost her first husband, sister and mother to cancer, she was frustrated with interviewers expecting her to be miserable. 'Some see me as a tragic heroine … The idea I might be happy is unforgivable. Well I'm sorry, it's better to be happy.' And the simple truth is that it is.

Choose to be happy.
It's the only sensible option!

The **First Key** is all about making strong positive choices in life. Any time you find yourself blaming someone else for a situation or circumstance in your life, ask yourself, 'What choice am I making; how am I a co-contributor here?' Apply the *principle of choice*; examine your decisions and if they are not working for you, **take charge** of your life and make new ones.

Let It Go

The Principle of Acceptance

The desire for control is one of the biggest causes of stress and unhappiness in people's lives; however, the majority of the time the very idea that you are the one in control is an illusion. If you live in a bubble or on a mountaintop where you never have to come into contact with another person, you might manage some semblance of control over your life, but it's unlikely if you live in the modern world.

There are very few things in life you can actually control and accepting this is one of the keys to lifelong happiness. You can't control the weather. You can't control whether your train runs on time, your flight is delayed or you get stuck in a traffic jam. You can't control the people around you, the way your partner behaves or the way your children turn out.

So many of life's eventualities are beyond your control. Work out what things you can influence and come to a peaceful acceptance of the rest.

Why complain when the weather report says it is going to rain when you've planned a day at the beach? Complaining isn't going to make a spot of difference, except of course ruining a perfectly good day for watching a DVD on the sofa or going for a leisurely lunch.

How often have you raged at the response you've received from someone in a call centre, or, worse, at the automated voice that answered your call? You may not agree with the voice on the end of the line, and I know firsthand how frustrating or impractical they can seem, but is it really worth sacrificing your happiness and inviting distress into your life?

Trains, planes and automobiles? All out of your control. The best thing is to plan for the eventualities that so often occur: leave a little earlier, take a good book or phone a friend.

You need to choose your battles wisely. If your goal is to live in a state of happiness, where you are content and fulfilled the majority of the time, you need to be wise about avoiding things that threaten this state. I remind my clients that a great warrior like Sun Tzu or Machiavelli would never send an army into a losing battle and, given that you are personally unlikely to be at war right now, the resources you need to protect are your emotional ones: your capacity for stress, disappointment, frustration, anxiety or hurt. Throughout life you will have experiences that result in some if not all of these emotions, but why *invite* them into your life?

Every time you willingly fight a losing battle, that is exactly what you are doing: welcoming stress and unhappiness into your life. Before you embark upon your next crusade, ask yourself, 'What are my real chances? Do I have more than an eighty per cent chance of victory or am I fighting a battle that wisdom, history and past experience tell me I am unlikely to win?' If you think you are in with a good chance and that the reward will be worth the effort, then go for it. But if that is not the response you come up with, you need to have a good, honest think about what it is really about. If your decision is driven by the desire to be proven right, you might want to ask yourself if there are easier ways you can stroke your ego and if your self-esteem is likely to benefit if you come off second best.

Choose your battles wisely. Unless you have a very high chance of victory, spare your energy and walk away.

So often, people are drawn to losing battles because they feel infuriated and want things to be right 'because they should be'. While in a utopian world this would be a worthy goal, you really need to think about whether you're actually going to make a difference, and whether the difference you're likely to make is going to be worth your while.

I know I've given up doing battle with our telecommunications providers and other large conglomerates. I have come to a peaceful acceptance of the fact that they appear to be a law unto themselves. I've also accepted that regardless of which provider I'm with, I am likely to experience the same poor service, over-charging and general quality issues. So I stay put. Is this the right thing to do? In a black and white sense, of course it's not. But is it the right decision for me? Absolutely. I always ask myself, 'How important is this fight and do I have a good chance of winning? Will the emotional or financial gain outweigh the negativity this situation will bring into my life?' If my answer is no, the final question I always ask is, 'Am I going to be able to find peaceful acceptance of this situation?' There is no point in deciding not to fight if you are going to continue to complain. As the saying goes, put up or shut up.

However, sometimes there are battles that, while you may not feel confident you can win, you feel you must fight regardless. Perhaps you believe that even if you don't win, your contribution will be part of a larger effort, or maybe you feel that the only way to honour your values or moral code is to march on regardless. If this is the case, then fighting is most certainly the right thing to do. However, if you are to protect your sense of happiness and contentment, you need to focus your energy on the fact that you are fighting this battle to stand up and be counted and you must remove any attachment to victory. This doesn't mean you don't want to win. It just means that your happiness is not contingent on winning and that your sense of satisfaction and fulfilment will be achieved by knowing you fought a good fight.

Early on in my career I experienced exactly this kind of battle. My boss was a master of the art of extreme bullying, harassment and intimidation. Each time I raised my concern with my manager, and later the HR manager, I was told I needed to put up with the situation or find another job and that I should be grateful as a lot of other people would love to have my job. The stress of my boss's behaviour eventually became overwhelming and I began having physical symptoms including hair loss and stomach pains. When my GP suggested I go on sick leave, I decided enough was enough. This 'illness' had a very specific cause, so I went to see a lawyer.

Initially my lawyer felt I most definitely had a case and, as I had kept a detailed diary of incidents and correspondence, it shouldn't be too difficult to prove, but when I told him who my employer was, he baulked. The organisation I was working for had diplomatic immunity. That meant unless an employee committed a capital crime, such as murder, manslaughter or something equally gruesome, they could not be held accountable for their actions in a court of law.

My lawyer agreed it was an outrage that an organisation could be exempt in this way. He believed not only that I had a moral right to fight my employer, but also that it was my human right. He sat me down and explained that while if I were working for anyone else, I would have a very good case, in this situation we would first have to win the right to make a case … in the Court of Human Rights. He felt that we at best had a fifty-fifty chance of winning this first suit, but he was happy to waive his normally huge fees as he knew we would change history if we won. For me it was not about any history other than my own. I wanted to stand up and say, 'I was treated this way and it wasn't okay. It shouldn't have happened to me and it shouldn't happen to anyone else'. I knew the odds weren't good but I decided to pursue the case regardless.

We didn't win. After twelve months of tribunals, courts and appeals the time came to accept that my employer's immunity would not be waived and I would not be given the chance to bring my case to court.

Although it was disappointing, I had wisely *engaged* myself in the fight, but *detached* myself from the outcome. I soon realised that I had won all I needed to win, many months before. I was still an employee the day the legal papers were served. All I had ever wanted to say was, 'Your behaviour was NOT okay', and the look on my boss's face when he received his summons told me my message had been received loud and clear. It had been an incredible journey, and despite losing the legal battle, I knew I had made myself heard, which was victory enough for me.

When you are focused on *having* control, it is easy to forget life is a road you are travelling, not a destination you get to. Letting go and detaching yourself from outcomes you can't control makes it easier to enjoy your experiences for what they are, what you have gained and what you have learned.

Don't be attached to outcomes. Enjoy your experiences for what they are, what you have gained and what you have learned.

Any goal that you set is an intention to achieve a certain result, in a given time frame. Unless you have a crystal ball you don't know how the future is going to unfold, yet often I find when people don't achieve their goal they consider themselves to have failed, or, worse, think they are a failure. If you are able to detach yourself from the outcome, it is much easier to accept that while you did your best, not everything was within your control. You can then refocus your efforts on the things that you can influence.

Unless you have a crystal ball you don't know how the future is going to unfold. Focus on the things you can influence and don't fret over the rest.

Being the best you can be is not a competition. No one gets to get there first. Yet for so many people, instead of focusing on being the best they can be, they focus on being 'better than …' Better than him at this, better than her at that. They want to have more money, a bigger house, a fancier car, a better job and so on. Each time you compete in this way you are undermining your chances of happiness and eroding your self-esteem.

The Academy Award–winning actress Reese Witherspoon knows how foolish it is to compete. She told *Vanity Fair* magazine, 'There's no winning. You're

never going to win the thin race. You're never going
to win the pretty race. You're never going to win the
smart race. You're never going to win the funny race. I
just want to be the best version of myself I can be'. Wise
words indeed.

*Let go of the idea of winning
or losing. In the game of life,
the most important thing
is just showing up
and doing your best.*

The only person you should ever compete against is
yourself. We all have our own unique set of strengths
and weaknesses, our own positive qualities and those
attributes that don't do so much for us. Being the best
you can be is the only goal that really matters, so make
this the focus of your life and leave everyone else to
focus on their own goals.

Everyone makes their own choices, but when the person in question is a loved one, it can be hard to sit back and watch if you don't agree with those choices. Andrew was having a hard time with his daughter's choice of partner. In Andrew's own words, he wasn't so awful, he just didn't think he was right for her and he was worried an involvement with this man would bring her unhappiness in the long term.

When Andrew first spoke to me about this he was wondering how to bring this up with this daughter. He was looking for a way to say, 'I'm your dad and I'm not happy with your choice'. He wanted to change his daughter's mind about this man, and, being a loving father, he wanted to do it in a way that would cause as little conflict as possible.

Andrew did love his daughter, very much. He wasn't *trying* to be controlling, he was trying to ensure his daughter's happiness, but if Andrew was going to have a healthy relationship with his daughter he would need to accept that while he would always have a duty of care towards her, she was the only one responsible for her life.

When you are in a loving or caring relationship with an adult, you have a duty of care towards that person.

That means if there is something going on in their life that concerns you, you should express your concern, but you have no responsibility for any action or lack of action they may choose to take as a result of your concern. It is their life and it is up to them how they live it.

No matter how much you care about someone, you can't take responsibility for their happiness.

Of course, if you feel that the person you care about is genuinely unable to make healthy choices for themselves, such as in the case of an addiction or mental illness, or if they are at risk of harming themselves or others, part of your duty of care may be to take action on their behalf, but these are extreme cases.

When Andrew's daughter was young, he had a direct responsibility for her health, safety, and physical and emotional wellbeing. However, now that she was an adult she was free to make her own choices, pursue her own path and ultimately learn from her own mistakes.

When you care for someone, it's natural to want everything to be okay for them, but caring about someone doesn't make them your responsibility. In time, Andrew was able to shift his relationship with his daughter to one between two adults, where both have an equal duty of care towards each other. He is still concerned about his daughter from time to time, but he knows her happiness isn't his responsibility and he has found much of the weight of his stress and worry has lifted.

You can't *make* someone do what you want, or something that they don't want to do. This is true whether you are trying to get a job, fall in love or make your children clean up after themselves. You have no control over the other person's actions at all. What you do have, however, is the opportunity to influence the outcome.

Recognising your potential for influence is completely different from attempting to control a situation. If you are looking for a new job, you can influence the outcome by doing your research, tailoring your CV, being on time and well prepared for the interview and following up in a timely way. You can't make someone choose you for the job, but you can give yourself the best chance of being the selected candidate.

You can't make someone do something just because you want them to. What you do have, however, is the opportunity to influence their choices.

You can't make someone love you, but if you are looking for a partner, you can give yourself the best chance of finding the right person by meeting new people and being clear on what you are looking for: your negotiables, your non-negotiables and your relationship values. That way you will be able to recognise someone with genuine potential when they cross your path.

Anyone who has children will tell you they certainly have free will. You can't make your children do anything, but you can set a good example by modelling the behaviour you want them to adopt. You can encourage them with reward and you can reprimand or punish so they learn that *not* doing what you want will have consequences. When you exert your influence this way, you will get the outcome you desire at least *some* of the time. If you continually try to exert direct control you will only encourage resistance and rebellion. Even a small child doesn't like to feel that they are being forced to do something, and let's not even get started on teenagers!

The best way to influence any situation is to ask yourself, 'What is the outcome I am trying to achieve?' Unless you know what it is you *really* want, it is very hard to get it. So often I see people arguing one point only to find that it is another point altogether that really matters. One of my girlfriends tells the story of how arguments go between her and her partner. As she explains, 'He always wanted to be right and I always wanted to get my way. I found that as long as I agreed he was right, he usually agreed to what I wanted'. Of course she could have argued until she was blue in the face to get what she wanted, but she wisely realised that it was the outcome she was seeking, not the validation. It is a very happy relationship, so I can only assume her partner had realised he was seeking the validation and was less attached to the outcome.

The best way to get what you want from a situation is to have clarity about the outcome you want to achieve.

The same can be said for any conflict or challenging situation. Once you have defined your ideal outcome, you have something on which to focus your influence. And once you recognise that all you have is influence, not control, you can detach yourself from the outcome and ensure that your happiness is not dependent on it.

Your need to control a situation is a direct result of the strength of your self-esteem and part of what I call the Over-Achiever Syndrome. The more vulnerable your self-esteem, the more likely you will seek external validation of your worth and the more you will try to control the situation and its outcome to ensure you get that validation. The more robust your self-esteem the easier it is for your sense of self-worth to be self-referred; in other words, you can tell yourself how great you are, all on your own. High-achievers have robust self-esteem, they feel confident they did their best and they know their best is good enough. When you are an over-achiever you are always worried nothing you do will ever be good enough and so you try harder and harder to get the validation you crave. Over-achievers are rarely happy. They're usually perfectionists and control freaks, the least-detached people around!

When I talk about over-achievers, perfectionists and control freaks in my corporate speaking engagements, there is always a murmur of recognition among the audience. Invariably more than half the people in the room recognise themselves as someone whose self-esteem is dependent on the validation of others and who feels that they need to be in control of everything, all of the time, to give themselves the best chance of getting it. This means more than fifty per cent of my audience, and sometimes I am speaking to rooms of more than a thousand people, are actively getting in the way of their own happiness.

*Being a control freak
is a sign of a vulnerable
self-esteem. The better
you feel about yourself
the less you need to control
everything around you.*

The desire for control is like venom. It poisons any chance you have of experiencing continuous happiness in your life. The only thing you will ever have complete control over is the person you choose to be, so choose to be the best you can be.

The only thing you have total control over is who you choose to be. Be the best you can be.

The **Second Key** is all about letting go of your attachment to outcomes you can't control. Every time you find yourself getting angry or frustrated, ask yourself, 'What level of influence do I really have over this situation?' Apply the *principle of acceptance*; unless you are sure you have a strong degree of influence over the outcome, take a deep breath, **let it go** and disengage yourself from the source of your conflict.

Live for Now
The Principle of Presence

The most important moment of your life is this one.
Not yesterday or some golden heyday from your past.
Not tomorrow or some other time in the future when
you hope to achieve your goals. The only moment that
truly counts is the one you are living *right now*.

Being able to learn from the past is important.
Your past can hold so many answers about who you
are and why you think, feel or behave the way you do.
Understanding your past experiences can help you
to move forward in life and, armed with the lessons

you have learned, you can be more confident in your choices, stronger in your decisions and wiser about the path you are on.

Accept the past,
dream of the future,
but live in the moment.

A short visit to the past can be helpful when you are feeling stuck or looking for answers but if you linger in the past, it will only hold you back and prevent you from getting the most out of life. We all know someone who constantly complains about things that happened last week, last month or even last year. Perhaps you've been that person. The past is in the past and unless you own a time machine there is nothing you can do to change it, so don't waste your energy complaining about it. Accept the past for what it is, not what it could have been or what you wish it was, but simply what it is. Once you can leave the past where it firmly belongs, you can focus your energy towards creating the life you do want to be living and the person you want to become.

Living in the past is a direct barrier to happiness and one of the most effective ways you can remove this barrier is by recognising that nobody from your past is responsible for your future. I often hear adults blaming their parents for who they are or how their life has turned out. For most people the past contains a series of ups and downs but, even if your childhood really was truly horrible, it doesn't have to define who you are today. The same can be said if you have had a bad relationship where your trust was abused or, worse, you were. The best thing about the past is that it is where it should stay and regardless of what it was like, you don't have to be a prisoner to it in your future.

Learning from the past can help you move forward. Lingering in the past will only hold you back.

For some people, acting on this recognition is as simple as making the decision to let it go. For others, it may be more complicated and require the support of an expert: a counsellor or psychologist. If you think this might apply to you, act now and get the support you need to move on from your past and get on with your life.

Nobody from your past should be held responsible for your future. The only person accountable for your future is you.

Rebecca had a whole list of goals she wanted to achieve, covering a wide range of topics including travelling, buying a house and moving up the ladder at work. One of the goals on her list was to lose weight. Although Rebecca was a vibrant and energetic person, she was also seriously overweight. So much so that her weight was beginning to have an impact on her health and get in the way of some of her other goals.

After a few weeks of focusing on some of her other goals, Rebecca and I began to talk about her weight and how she wanted to return to a healthy BMI. I asked Rebecca if she had had any success with dieting or changing her eating habits in the past, as I wanted to understand a little more about the history of her weight problem, and see if there was anything that had supported her healthy eating habits in the past that she could apply this time round.

Rather than explain her success or lack of it in the past, Rebecca immediately launched into a passionate explanation of *why* she was overweight. In her mind her trouble with her weight had begun in her teens. While studying for her university entrance exams Rebecca had fallen into the habit of snacking on junk food and had put on a few kilograms. When Rebecca's mother noticed her weight gain she had said something along the lines of, 'You had better do something about that. Losing weight only gets harder as you get older and I don't want you to be fat'.

With the wisdom of hindsight, I hope Rebecca's mother would agree that this wasn't the most sensitive or supportive thing to say to a teenage girl. I'd like to give her the benefit of the doubt and assume her heart was in the right place but, regardless of what she was thinking, I'm sure it wasn't her intention that her daughter would spend the best part of the next twenty years in a cycle of binge eating that would take her from being a few kilos heavier than her ideal weight to becoming obese.

The more I probed Rebecca about her experiences, the more certain she became that *all* of her weight troubles had begun with this one comment from her mother. Perhaps at the time this comment had triggered a series of responses but, given that these comments had been made more than half her life ago, the real question was how much longer was Rebecca going to allow her mother's words to get in the way of a healthy, happy future.

The easiest way to determine if your past is getting in the way of your future is to examine the level of emotional energy you experience when you think about that time in your life. While you may remember feeling sad, hurt, angry or disappointed, if you are still actively experiencing those emotions chances are they are still holding you back and preventing you from moving forward in your life.

Rebecca hadn't consciously realised how much blame she had been attributing to this comment from the past and she had to acknowledge that *she* was the only one who was responsible for her food and exercise choices on a day-to-day basis.

This realisation allowed Rebecca to make a complete shift in the way she approached her diet and exercise goals. They were still a challenge, but they were now a challenge that she realised she alone had the power to meet. Slowly but surely Rebecca began to shed her excess weight, as well as the burden of being angry with her mother for all this time.

The Year of Magical Thinking, a memoir by Joan Didion, opens with the lines, 'Life changes fast. Life changes in the instant'. While she was writing of the sudden death of her husband, these lines are an important reminder to us all. Things can change suddenly and the life you have taken for granted could change in such a fundamental way that it is no longer recognisable to you. What a waste if you weren't even enjoying it.

I think of it as the 'hit-by-a-bus test'. If my life ended suddenly, would I be able to say I had been enjoying myself until that point? This isn't a question of whether or not my life was perfect or if I had done everything I wanted to do, been everywhere I wanted to go or bought everything I wanted to buy. It is simply a question of whether, if my life or quality of life were to end, I would feel content, fulfilled, happy with the life that I had been living up until that point.

It is important to try and find the joy in each and every day. It might not be immediately obvious but if you start each day reminding yourself how good it is to be alive, finding the reasons why this is true will start to come naturally to you.

Being confident you are happy in *this* moment is a good test of presence. Another is whether you can actually sit still and be present.

Look for the joy in each and every day. Just because it isn't immediately obvious, that doesn't mean it's not there.

As a child, if you were anything like me, you and your classmates were probably regularly told by your teachers to sit still and pay attention. Life is so exciting when you are a child and there are so many different things that capture your attention, which makes this a real challenge.

As adults, the information age we live in today makes sitting still and being present more of a challenge than ever. There are emails to read, tweets to send, pages to update, videos to watch, blogs to read, and they are all available to you all of the time. If that wasn't distracting enough, we are now all carrying around devices in our pockets or handbags that make this information overload a 24/7 problem, not just something to worry about during working hours. There are numerous strategies for managing this madness, but unless you disengage from the information available to you at least some of the time, it is very hard to relax and enjoy the moment.

Cast your mind back twenty years. Can you imagine watching two people sitting at the same table in a cafe, spending their time texting on their phone rather than speaking to each other? It wasn't that long ago that nobody but the CEO was expected to catch up with

their work correspondence at breakfast, in the evening
or any time outside nine-to-five. News broadcasts were
in the evening and if you missed one you could catch up
the following morning. Now perhaps I'm really showing
my age, but was it really that long ago that the focus of
family mealtimes was on conversation with each other?
The only potential interruption was the telephone,
but given that most people thought it was rude to call
during dinnertime, interruptions were unlikely.

*It's hard to be present when
your attention is suffering
information overload.
Switch off and just sit still.*

Interruptions seemed to be a constant feature in
Nick's life and at the end of each day he found himself
feeling guilty that he hadn't spent any quality time
with his twelve-year-old son. When I asked Nick about

mealtimes, he said that while he and his son often had breakfast at the same time they didn't use this time to chat. Like many people, Nick was too busy checking his emails, texting the office and catching up with the news on his laptop. He was trying to keep on top of so many things that he wasn't present to his son at all.

These challenges of modern life are unlikely to go away, so it is up to you to decide how to manage them. I suggested that if Nick wanted to spend a little more quality time with his son, he should keep his phone, BlackBerry and laptop away from the breakfast table and use that time to chat with his son. It is a sad sign of the times that this idea seems revolutionary.

To me it's simple. Be there when you're there.

I was recently asked at a workshop I was running how I was able to manage all the different roles in my life: coaching my clients, training other coaches, writing books and speaking at conferences, all the while being a good wife and caring and supportive mother. Didn't I feel guilty and torn all the time? The truth is I don't. I juggle all these roles by not juggling them at all. I always aim to make whatever role I am called to at the time the only role I am playing. I'm not going to lie to you; I'm not perfect and of course I slip up sometimes, but my intention is to always give one hundred per cent of my attention to the role I am in at that time.

Be there when you are there. Don't try to juggle all the roles in your life. Focus on the role you are playing and do it to the best of your ability.

If I am with my daughter, I avoid taking work calls or replying to emails and if I'm at work, I give my clients all of my attention without worrying about whether or not my daughter liked what she had for lunch. When I am writing I clear my diary and if I am on holiday the sign says 'do not disturb'.

It's not about being perfect; it's about being the best you can be, and one of the easiest ways you can offer the people in your life the best version of you is to be present to them when you are with them. Stop trying to type an email while talking on the phone. Turn the TV off or put your book down if someone is trying to speak with you, and simply don't answer the phone if you are not going to give the person at the other end of the line the attention they deserve.

Multi-tasking will only make you miserable and increase the stress in your life, so instead focus on a single task. Do it to the best of your ability and when it is complete, move on to the next thing. Taking this approach doesn't mean you have to get in the slow lane. You will find you get things done much faster if you focus on them one at a time, and you will find all the things you need to do feel less of a burden when you are not trying to do them all at once.

*Multi-tasking is stressful.
You will get things done
much faster if you do them
one at a time.*

Living in the moment also means that you stop wasting your life away dreaming of the future. I am a passionate believer in the importance of having a vision, setting goals and creating a plan to help you to achieve them. But it is important not to give so much of your attention to the future that you don't enjoy your life as it is.

When you do achieve one of your goals, you need to stop, take a deep breath and appreciate your achievement for all that it is worth, not immediately rush on to the next step in your plan.

Having a vision is great,
but don't be so focused on
your next goal that you forget
to enjoy your achievements.

Martha, the founder of a rapidly expanding chain of coffee shops, was fuelled by an entrepreneur's drive for constant change, quick results and the kind of success you could touch and see. During one particular coaching session, Martha was feeling down and not her usual energetic self. She explained how the lease on potential new premises had fallen through and after all the work that had gone into getting it to this stage, her plans would now be put back at least three months. She was feeling really frustrated because she wasn't going to achieve *anything*.

Martha was so busy focusing on the next step in her plan, the next shop she was going to open and the next store manager she was going to hire, that she was failing to see her business for the success it already was. When Martha made a list of all she had achieved in the last twelve months, she was astonished. Whenever she'd achieved a goal, she'd been so quick to move on to the next stage of her plan that she never stopped to acknowledge her achievements and to enjoy her success in those moments.

Looking towards the future, and having a plan for how you would like things to unfold, is one of the great delights in life, as long as you are not so focused on the life you are *going to* create that you don't enjoy the one you already have.

*Nobody's life is perfect.
Rather than wishing
for things you don't have,
make the most of the
things you do have.*

Every day we are all bombarded by advertising messages designed to make us feel that what we have isn't good enough or that our life is inadequate in some way. At the same time we are socially and culturally conditioned to expect our life to look a certain way. As children we are read fairytales and told our prince will come (or that we'll find a princess to rescue) and advertisers begin to tell us from a very young age that if we don't buy a big castle, with shiny appliances and a new car in the driveway, and have our 2.2 kids, a cat and a dog, then we really can't expect to live happily ever after. These messages might be fine at bedtime when you're a child, but do you really want to accept this nonsense, from either the brothers Grimm or the media, now you are an adult?

Samantha had a rewarding job, a beautiful home and great friends. The one thing she wanted that she didn't have was a baby. Until this point in her life, Samantha had been able to buy anything that she felt she wanted, but that wasn't really an option in this case and her desire for what was *missing* from her life began to consume her. She saw her friends with children as having perfect lives and saw her own as being deeply flawed, and she found herself resenting her friends with children and feeling angry that her life hadn't turned out like theirs.

Despite her mixed feelings, Samantha adored her friends' children and when the opportunity came to babysit one of them for a week while the mother was in hospital having her second child, she jumped at the chance. By the end of the week Samantha was completely frazzled. She had been swept away by the romance of being a parent, the unconditional love and endless joy, and she hadn't fully comprehended the thankless work that went with it.

Even in that short time, Samantha's eyes were opened to the realities of having a child and she realised that the lives of her friends with children weren't so perfect after all. They were tired all the time and stressed from juggling the demands of their jobs and their responsibilities as parents. They had lost a significant amount of their disposable income and practically all of their freedom and flexibility. Samantha finally believed those friends who had confessed that while they loved their children dearly, they were more than a tiny bit envious of her fun-filled life.

Samantha still dearly wanted to have a child of her own, and ideally a partner to have that child with, but she realised her life wasn't actually that bad. She didn't know what the future held, so she made the commitment to enjoying the present and getting as much enjoyment out of her single and carefree life as she could, for as long as it lasted.

Aspiration can be a great motivator as long as you are not so focused on what you don't have that it makes you unhappy. If you fall into this trap, you miss a great opportunity to enjoy your life as it is. You might want to do some home improvements or to move house, to buy new shoes or to lose that baby weight, to get a promotion or to start your family. You may have all of these things in your future and feel that your life has been enhanced because of them, but to allow your happiness to be restricted because they are not yet present is nothing more than a waste … a waste of the opportunity to enjoy the life you have today.

It's okay to aspire to a better life, but don't let it stop you from enjoying the life you already have.

The **Third Key** is all about enjoying the life you have. Make a commitment to enjoy each and every moment for what it is. Don't form attachments or make criticisms about what was and don't try to presuppose what might be. Apply the *principle of presence*; remind yourself that things simply are what they are. **Live for now**— appreciate each moment for the experience it offers.

Expect the Best

The Principle of Optimism

When you wake up each morning, how do you expect your day to turn out? Do you jump out of bed, excited about the prospect of another day, or do you pull the pillow over your head and think, 'Oh no, here we go again'? The energy with which you start each day will have a fundamental impact on the way your day turns out. Jumping out of bed is optional (I know, I'm not a morning person) but looking forward to the coming day is essential if you want to regularly experience the kind of day that brings joy and happiness into your life.

Your expectations in life will determine your experience of life. If you expect your day to be a good one, it probably will be. And if you expect your life to be good, it, too, probably will be. Optimism, or positive expectation, is one of the most important contributors to experiencing continuous happiness.

Unless you have a crystal ball, at the start of each day you have no way of knowing how your day is going to turn out. It could be an amazing day, filled with wonder and delight; it could be an awful day, where nothing goes right at all; or, as is most often the case, your day will turn out just fine. It may not be perfect, but on balance it will still be pretty good, so why not begin each day expecting nothing less?

Your expectations determine
your experience.
Expect the best from life
and you will usually get it.

If you want to be happy, you need to stop expecting the worst and then worry that it's going to happen. To quote *Chicago Tribune* journalist Mary Schmich, whose words were later used by Baz Luhrmann in the song 'Everybody's Free (To Wear Sunscreen)': 'Don't worry about the future. Or worry, but know that worrying is as effective as trying to solve an algebra equation by chewing bubble gum'. It sounds like such simple advice, but I meet so many people who spend so much energy worrying about what *might* happen that they don't have any energy left to enjoy what usually *does* happen.

Worrying is a complete waste of time and energy. It has no positive effect on the outcome and is nothing more than an unproductive habit, a habit you have created and one you need to break. You might think that you have no choice but to worry, that you are a worrier or that the circumstances of your life warrant worry and consternation. The truth is, while these concerns may deserve *consideration*, you would be better placed moving the energy you would normally spend worrying to doing something about the things that concern you.

*Worrying doesn't change anything.
Focus your energy on the outcome
you do want and then do what
you can to make it happen.*

The things that worry you will most likely fall into
one of two categories: things you can do something
about, and things that, as much as you would like to be
able to do something about, you just can't. The best use
of your energy is to *do something* about those things
you can and accept the rest.

If you can adopt an optimistic approach in your
life, it becomes much easier not to worry. When
your expectation is for a positive outcome, instead
of worrying about what might go wrong, you simply
assume that it will go right.

Jason was at a career crossroads. He had recently
been headhunted by a competitor to set up a new
division. It was an exciting opportunity and while Jason

wasn't unhappy in his current job he knew that he would welcome the challenge of working on something new. However, what Jason also knew was that he really enjoyed the status and recognition he had received at his current firm. He had a reputation for being one of the best salespeople in the company and he was worried about losing the reputation he had worked for and having to start all over again.

When Jason and I began to talk about his career options, it quickly became apparent that the shift in status wasn't the only thing he was worried about. He was worried about whether he would like his new colleagues and whether or not they would like him. He worried that he might not hit his sales targets and that he might not like the team members that were in place. He was worried that if he didn't succeed at this new job he might be fired at the end of his probation and that if he did succeed at the job, the hours might be really long. There really wasn't much Jason wasn't worried about and if he continued to put all his energy into expecting the worst, he might just get it!

I began to challenge Jason on his expectations and what the likelihood was that his fears would become a reality. When pushed, Jason had to admit that it was unusual for him not to get along with colleagues, that the targets his new company had set were not unreasonable and that while he was going to be new to this company, he was joining them nowhere near the bottom of the ladder; in fact, his reputation would actually precede him … that was why he'd been headhunted in the first place.

Jason realised his worries really were a waste of energy and although there were risks involved in this new job, the most likely outcome was that he would succeed. He had succeeded at new challenges in the past and there was no valid reason to think this new job would be any different, and he decided to focus his energy on this point: on the positive expectation that his new job would be brilliant.

When you go though life expecting only good things to happen to you, it's much easier to keep a smile on your face and a spring in your step. You will find that you always have an abundance of energy because you are no longer wasting it worrying and on the unfortunate occasion that things don't go your way, you will be able to use some of that energy you have been saving to deal with it.

*Most of the things that go wrong
in life don't have a lasting impact.
Remind yourself that if it won't
matter in ten years' time,
it doesn't matter today.*

Even when things do go wrong, the majority of
the time they won't have a lasting impact on your life.
Perhaps you've failed an exam, been stood up on a date
or been passed over for a promotion. Although things
can be upsetting at the time, when you are optimistic
it is much easier to see how little impact today's
disappointments are likely to have on your life as a
whole and you are able to remind yourself, 'If it won't
matter in ten years' time, it doesn't matter today'.

When you are an optimist, you focus your *attention*
on your *intention*, the outcome you would most like to
create, and by focusing on this you are more likely to

see the possibilities of making this intention a reality. You've probably heard the expression that the harder you work, the luckier you get. It is very similar with optimism: the more optimistic you are, the more luck you will discover. As Winston Churchill said, 'A pessimist sees the difficulty in every opportunity; an optimist sees the opportunity in every difficulty'.

When you see the world as being filled with positive potential, you are much more likely to see how those possibilities might be able to serve you, rather than seeing a potential opportunity and thinking, 'Oh well, that will never happen to me'. Instead you are able to seize the moment and just go for it.

See the world as being filled with positive potential. Focus your attention on your intention and make that potential a reality in your life.

If your expectations are positive, you are more likely to take a chance or give things a go. Why not apply for that new job, why not pitch that new idea, why not ask her out on a date, why not put in an offer on your dream home? Why not indeed!

By the same token, optimists are also happy to create opportunities for themselves. Melanie was a journalist who wrote new product reviews for a supermarket magazine. She was an excellent writer and had even completed her MA in creative writing, but she graduated right in the middle of a recession and so, being happy to have a job, any job, she ended up writing for the supermarket. At the time she told herself she would just stay until the job market picked up, but that was four years ago and here she was, still writing about new jams and different ways to pack school lunches. It wasn't that she didn't like writing about food; she did, but writing about food in this way wasn't exactly challenging and it was starting to get her down.

Melanie knew something had to change, but she wasn't sure what or how. She thought perhaps she could start writing some feature articles for the magazine focusing on the people aspect of food creation: the growers, manufacturers, chefs and so on. It sounded like a great idea. But as soon as Melanie started focusing on her idea in more detail, all of her doubts came into play. Her editor probably wouldn't go for it, people might not want to be interviewed and her interview technique might be so rusty that she wouldn't be any good anyway.

When I asked Melanie what she would do if she knew she couldn't fail, her answer was clear. She would be a food writer at *Vogue* magazine. No sooner were the words out of her mouth than she began thinking of all the reasons why this wasn't possible. Why would *Vogue* take on someone like her, how would she survive on less money (*Vogue* may have been more prestigious but it actually paid less than the more commercial environment that she was in) and, of course, what if she submitted an article and they told her it was rubbish? Would she ever recover from the humiliation, and would she suffer writer's block forever more?

I asked Melanie to take her thinking one step further. How would she go about making this a reality in her life, if her success was one hundred per cent guaranteed? Again her answer was clear; she had obviously given it a lot of thought. She would submit a pitch for an article as a freelancer and then when it was picked up she would write it in the evenings and at the weekends. Even though it would mean a lot of extra work, she would keep working this way until she was commissioned to write enough articles to resign from her current job.

When you shift your focus from what might go wrong to what could go right, you have a far greater chance of making the outcome you desire a reality in your life. When Melanie focused on a positive outcome, she realised that the worst thing that could really happen was that her story pitch might not be picked up and that she would fail. I suggested that she re-frame this sense of potential failure to this: 'The worst that can happen is that I won't succeed *this time* ...' and to embrace the positive expectancy that she would, in time, succeed.

Don't be afraid to take a chance. The worst that can happen is that you don't succeed ... this time.

Being able to see the positive potential of any situation is a real skill and although it may come more naturally to some than others, I firmly believe that, like any skill, it can be learned. Too many people focus their energy on the worst that might happen in any given situation. While understanding the risks of any situation can be valuable information, allowing you to put plans in place to manage or mitigate those risks, putting all your focus on what can go wrong all but eliminates your chance of happiness. Being an optimist doesn't mean you are blind to the reality of a situation. An optimist doesn't say that nothing bad can ever happen. An optimist simply says it is *most likely* that good things will happen.

Being an optimist is not about ignoring consequences. Understanding the potential consequences of a situation can be very helpful in managing the outcome to your advantage. When you know what can go wrong, it's much easier to make things go right.

No matter how optimistic you are, sometimes life still throws you a curve ball. Helen was someone everyone would agree was a vibrant and positive person. She was one of those people who appeared to have her life completely sorted. She was in a job she loved, had a great partner, was fit and healthy and was living in her dream apartment. Then she received the heartbreaking news that her partner's father had cancer and it was terminal.

Being optimistic isn't about believing nothing can go wrong. An optimist acknowledges what can go wrong but expects things to go right.

At the time Helen and her partner were living overseas, but after a lot of thought and consideration, they decided to move back home so her partner could spend more time with his father in his final months. The doctors anticipated he had about a year to live so Helen and her partner packed up their life and moved home from the other side of the world. In true Helen style, no sooner had they made this decision than she had created a plan for the next year of her life. She was determined to make this change a positive one and had a study goal, to complete her Masters through Open University; a fitness goal, to compete in a triathlon; and a goal for every other aspect of her life. Helen was determined to turn this situation into a positive change in her life.

I didn't speak to Helen for a few weeks while she packed up and attended to the physical move, and when we spoke again it was as if I was speaking to a very different person. Helen was feeling very low and miserable. She said she couldn't understand why she was feeling so bad when she had all these great goals she was looking forward to achieving. This was supposed to be a positive change and she was a positive person and she wondered what was going wrong.

But being an optimist and having a positive expectancy isn't about being naive or blind to the reality of a situation. Regardless of whether it's a terminal diagnosis, the end of a relationship or a redundancy, some things in life are tough. They can be upsetting, confronting, challenging or distressing. Being optimistic is not about denying yourself these emotions; instead, an optimist acknowledges that as upset, confronted, challenged or distressed as they are right now, this time will eventually pass, and that regardless of their experience in *this* moment, ultimately their life will still be a good one.

Remember, however bad things might be right now, this moment will pass and your life will continue to be a good one.

Helen realised she had been ignoring the reality that her father-in-law's diagnosis was a dreadful thing and packing up the life she had loved was the last thing she had wanted to do. Her immediate reality was sad and upsetting and in her desire to be positive she had been denying herself the opportunity to experience these emotions.

Once Helen acknowledged that she had been forcing herself to be positive, she began to feel much better.

She was still sad for all the reasons we had discussed, but now that she was allowing herself to experience this sadness instead of bottling it up, she actually felt energised. She admitted things were pretty awful right now, but the optimist in her could see that in time she would feel good about her life again. She would need to grieve for her father-in-law and for the life she had sacrificed but she could see that despite these changes in her life, her life would always be a good one.

Being an optimist is not about being falsely positive or forcing yourself to smile brightly when you feel like crying. It is about being able to smile *through* your tears and, in the words of Orphan Annie, remembering that 'The sun'll come out tomorrow'.

Don't deny your emotions and force yourself to smile when you feel like crying. Cry, but learn to smile through your tears.

Being optimistic doesn't mean that you don't acknowledge things can go wrong. Unlike someone who is trying to force themselves to only think positive thoughts, an optimist is quite comfortable fully exploring *all* the potential consequences of a situation: the good, the bad and the ugly. An optimist will explore the worst-case scenario and make sure that they feel confident they can manage even their least-desired potential outcome. Once they are aware of the potential downsides of a situation, they can relax and anticipate the upside.

Not everybody wants to be optimistic. Some people, consciously or subconsciously, revel in their negative perspective, believing that the world is a horrible place, expecting the worst and feeling vindicated when they get it. We all know someone who likes to squash every idea with all the reasons why it can't be done, who tells you all the reasons why you are likely to fail before you've even begun and who firmly believes that every silver lining has a big black cloud hanging over it.

Negative people are entitled to their perspective as long as they keep it to themselves. Unfortunately, sharing their viewpoint with the world seems to be something negative people just love to do. Fine if you can ignore them, but much tougher if that person is a fixture in your life. If a family member, loved one, colleague or client is constantly being negative, you need to make sure that their perspective doesn't corrupt yours. Remind yourself that their viewpoint is theirs alone and just because it is something they passionately believe, that doesn't mean you have to share their passion. Rather than engage with this person in a heated debate about whose perspective is right, protect yourself from their negativity by not engaging with them on the subject at all.

You need to be mindful of the company you keep. If the person who is negative is someone you can't avoid, then you need to develop strategies for dealing with them so that their negativity doesn't wear you down, but if that person is a friend and someone you have *chosen* to have in your life, you may need to have a think about why. The saying goes, 'people come into your life for a reason, a season or a lifetime', and sometimes friendships that may have formed because of a common interest or shared circumstance, or maintained on account of their history, have simply passed their expiry date. Perhaps you were willing to overlook a friend's negativity when you were both the new people at work or you had to grin and bear it because they were friends with your ex. Maybe you have been friends since you sat next to each other in school and your friendship is based on sharing the same first letter of your surname, not common values and ideas. If you find the people you are choosing to surround yourself with are constantly bringing you down, it is probably time to expand your horizons and discover a new circle of friends.

Be mindful of the company you keep. Don't let negative people cloud your vision.

Expecting the best doesn't mean having unrealistic expectations of yourself. Expecting yourself to succeed at something new the first time you try it, that you can drop ten kilos in a week or that you can cram for an exam and still get an 'A', will only cause you stress and frustration. When you are optimistic you set yourself up for success, not failure, by ensuring that while your expectations are positive, they are not naive or foolish.

There is a big difference between having a positive expectation of yourself and being a perfectionist. A perfectionist is always striving for an unattainable goal and spends a lot of their time feeling miserable because they have failed. Expecting the best from yourself is about striving to be the best you can be and knowing that as long as you give your best, your best is good enough.

Perfection is impossible. Expecting the best from yourself isn't about trying to be perfect; it's about striving to be the best you can be.

The **Fourth Key** is all about the way you believe life is likely to turn out. Each time you begin something new, ask yourself, 'What are my expectations?' To succeed at your goal you need to ensure your expectations are authentically positive. Apply the *principle of optimism*; **expect the best** from yourself and your life.

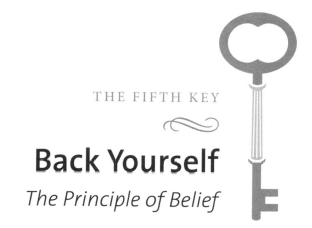

Back Yourself

The Principle of Belief

When you think about your life, do you believe you *can* be happy, you *will* be happy and you *deserve* to be happy? Having a sense of belief in yourself, in your dreams and in your right to pursue and achieve those dreams, is essential if you are to have a full and meaningful life. You need to know unequivocally that to have the things you want in life is not only a perfectly reasonable expectation, but something that you truly deserve.

So many people, when hearing of the good fortune of others, say, 'But that will never happen to me'. But why couldn't it happen to you, and, more importantly, why shouldn't it?

Believe in yourself, believe in your dreams and believe in your right to achieve your dreams.

One of the most significant contributors to the level of happiness you experience is your *life paradigm*. Your life paradigm is your fundamental belief-set or operating model for your life. Put simply, it's how you see things working or not working in your life.

The happiest people operate with a life paradigm similar to, 'My life will be great. Good things will regularly happen for me. On the rare occasion when things don't go my way or when tough times occur, I will be able to cope and I will emerge stronger for the experience'. Is your life paradigm similar to this or does it need a little work? Are you someone who looks forward to moving through life with ease, or do you believe life needs to be tough in order to be meaningful, or operate with the expectation that life will always be hard? Do you see yourself as someone who is lucky and deserving of love, or as someone who expects to be disappointed by life?

Your life paradigm is the set of beliefs or operating system for your life. Make sure you choose one that supports lifelong happiness.

Anita worked at an agency that booked hairdressers, make-up artists and photographers for fashion shoots. Although she found her job incredibly stressful when it was busy, she loved working on this side of the fashion industry.

Anita and I discussed several strategies she could apply for balancing some of the stress she felt when the phones were ringing like crazy, but after a couple of coaching sessions it became apparent that Anita felt just as stressed when she wasn't busy. Anita also felt stressed when she accompanied a client to an assignment and stressed when she stayed back at the office, stressed when she was asked to recommend a make-up artist and stressed when the client had a fixed idea of who they wanted. It seemed anything and everything about her work stressed her out.

While Anita hadn't given any thought to the concept of a life paradigm, she readily admitted that she believed that all good jobs came with a fair deal of stress attached, and that she believed people who didn't find their jobs stressful probably weren't committed enough to them.

No wonder Anita was stressed all the time. Not only did she believe her job *had* to be stressful, she also believed that if she wasn't finding it stressful then she didn't care enough. No stress management technique was going to make a difference to Anita's stress levels until she addressed her fundamental belief that work needed to be stressful.

Anita was reluctant at first. These were deep-seated and long-held beliefs, and she found the thought of giving them up confronting. If work wasn't meant to be stressful and she didn't have to feel stressed in order to demonstrate her commitment, then what was work supposed to feel like, and how was she supposed to show how good she was and how much she cared?

Despite how it may feel, your life paradigm is something you can choose. You might start out with one you have adopted from your parents or other social influences, but as an intelligent adult you are entirely free to *choose* the operating model for your life. And, given that it is a choice, you may as well choose to believe that your life is going to be truly wonderful and that any time it doesn't feel that way, these are simply pebbles on the road to true contentment and happiness in your life.

Anita decided to experiment with a new paradigm, one where work gave her enormous pleasure and where her contribution was always valued and her commitment always recognised. After a couple of weeks of 'trialling' her new set of beliefs, Anita could see how much of an impact it had had on her happiness. It was easy to let go of so much of the stress she had been experiencing once she realised she didn't need to feel that way and that stress wasn't an essential component of her job description.

Unless you adopt a life paradigm that supports a state of continued happiness, it will always be difficult to experience it in your life. If you expect things to be difficult, that will usually be the experience you will have, and if you expect life's occasional challenges to be something you can manage, then that too will be the case.

Anita still loves her job, but these days when she speaks of her job, it is without the exhaustion and burden of constant stress and instead with the joy and elation of someone who knows what a pleasure it is to have a job you truly love.

Your self-esteem is a valuable resource. Make sure you encourage, nurture, protect and support yours.

Regardless of what you want to achieve from life, from the humblest goals to the most audacious, the first person who needs to believe in them is you. And in order to believe in your goals, the first thing you have to do is believe in yourself.

Having a healthy level of self-belief is an essential contributor to lifelong happiness. It helps you to see your goals, dreams and ideas as having the potential to be a reality in your life. Just as we need wholesome food and exercise to make our bodies strong, our self-belief needs positive reinforcement and encouragement to grow. Although many parents are wise enough today to make developing their children's sense of self-worth a priority, this hasn't always been the case. Until relatively recently it wasn't something the average parent gave much thought to. But even if your parents were relics from the 'spare the rod and spoil the child' or the 'children should be seen and not heard' eras, or, worse, if their own negative experiences left them ill-equipped to provide you with a positive one, you can still learn to believe in yourself now.

One of the most important things you can do to boost your self-belief is to start listening to your internal conversations and self-talk. How do you speak to yourself? Are you your own biggest fan or your harshest critic? Are you your own best cheerleader, cheering yourself on regardless of whether it looks

like you are on the winning team, or are you the first
to berate yourself when things don't go according
to plan?

*Regardless of your upbringing or
formative experiences, it is never too
late to start believing in yourself.*

Not so long ago I was in the park with my daughter.
To me parenting is one of life's greatest privileges. Every
day I remind myself how blessed I am to have my
daughter in my life, so you can imagine my shock when
the following scene unfolded.

At first I couldn't work out what was going on. I
could hear a child whimpering as if he was hurt or
afraid, but I couldn't see him. And then I heard his
mother calling out, 'Don't be so pathetic, you're such a
big scaredy-cat, of course you can climb down the tree
… you got up, didn't you?' I looked up and there he
was in the tree. He wasn't up that high, but given that

he was only six or seven it was still more than twice his height. Not being such a big fan of heights myself, I could more than understand his hesitation.

His mother started to raise her voice and continued to tell her son how pathetic he was, how foolish it was of him to be scared, how his friends could all do it and how everyone was going to laugh at him. On and on it went. By now the boy was sobbing and I was starting to feel very uncomfortable with what I was hearing. The scene finally ended when a friend of the mother's came over and intervened, telling her enough was enough and helping the boy out of the tree.

'You're pathetic, I can't believe you couldn't do it, everyone will laugh at you, don't be so ridiculous ...' We all know that is no way to speak to a child and yet, how often do you find that you speak to yourself like that? How often do you criticise your efforts, judge yourself for not succeeding at the first attempt, or berate and tell yourself what a fool you are?

Every time we interact with a child we are, in that moment, the guardian of their self-esteem. As adults we are the guardians of our own. You don't have to be a parent to know how destructive that woman's behaviour was to her son's sense of self-belief. It's easy to imagine how small and worthless this little boy was feeling by the time his mother's friend took him down from the tree, but how often do you speak to yourself in a way that only leaves you feeling small and worthless? Never speak to yourself more harshly than you would to a small child.

Examine your self-talk. Never speak to yourself more harshly than you would to a small child.

What this mother should have said to her son was something along the lines of, 'I know you're scared, but I really think you can do it. It looks tough, but take a deep breath and try to be brave. I'll be here to catch you if you fall. I believe in you and I believe you can do it'.

This is exactly how you should be speaking to yourself: encouraging, nurturing, and building confidence and self-belief.

If this little boy decided, despite his mother's encouragement, that today wasn't to be his day, she could have said to him, 'Don't worry, you can't always master something the first time you try it; no big deal, let's come back tomorrow and try again'. When was the last time you were this kind to yourself when you didn't get something right the first time? Your self-belief is something to be encouraged, nurtured, supported and protected.

The happiest, most successful people believe in themselves unconditionally. They know they can do, be and have all that they want in life.

The happiest people believe in themselves unconditionally. They believe they can do, be and have all that they want from life and they support and encourage themselves to get it … without a boot camp sergeant in sight!

It's easy to feel good about yourself when someone is telling you how good you are. But if your self-belief and sense of self-worth are dependent on other people's belief in you, you can't expect yourself to feel good when those words are not forthcoming.

One of the greatest gifts you can give yourself is self-belief, with as much emphasis on the word 'self' as there is on 'belief'. Not everything in life can be counted to go your way. It may be that you miss out on getting the job you wanted, get dumped when you thought you were in love, lose what you thought was a winning pitch, miss out on an invitation to an event you were hoping to attend or get turned down by the bank for a loan for your new business. Regardless of what is going on in your life, it is important not to let it have an impact on your self-belief. If your belief is dependent on the approval or reinforcement of others, then every time something doesn't go your way, your self-esteem will be left battered and bruised. When you believe in yourself unconditionally, your self-esteem is independent of the opinions of others and it won't matter what anyone else says or thinks. Just because you didn't get the job or didn't win a pitch, that doesn't mean that you or your ideas don't have great potential. If a relationship ends unexpectedly, it doesn't mean that you aren't a great catch, and if someone doesn't think to include you, it's their loss, not yours.

Don't depend on others to fuel your self-belief. Develop your self-belief so that it becomes self-sustaining.

Winston Churchill once said, 'Success is the ability to go from one failure to another with no loss of enthusiasm'. When your self-belief is a self-sustaining resource, it will not be vulnerable to the whims of others. The more robust your self-esteem, the easier it will be for you to take the ups and downs, knock-backs and setbacks in your stride, confident that your happiness is not dependent on anyone or anything other than yourself.

Sometimes it is the people we love most who are not able to believe in our goals and dreams the way we do. This isn't because they love us any less, but because their own goals, hopes and dreams, as well as their fears, self-doubts and limiting beliefs, get in the way: the best friend who doesn't want you to move overseas because she will miss you, the mate who talks down your new job because he knows you will be earning more than him, or the partner who thinks your new goals will leave you with less time for them.

When you believe in yourself it is easier not to take criticism, knock-backs and disappointments personally.

Peter is one of the most ambitious and hard-working men I know. He was focused on expanding his business without compromising his values. As well as his business ambitions, he was committed to keeping fit and healthy, and being a great husband and a loving father to his two young daughters.

Peter's business was going from strength to strength but he didn't want to compromise his precious 'daddy time' with his girls, so he made sure that he left the office on time every night to get home in time to read them their bedtime stories. After a quick dinner with his wife, he was back at his computer working away until late at night. While Peter's wife didn't love the evenings he spent at his laptop, she understood that was what was needed for the business to grow and that the alternative was for him to stay at the office and for the girls to miss out on their time with their dad.

Although technically small in staff numbers, Peter's business was competing against much larger companies and an opportunity arose for them to expand into the much sought after American market. If the business was successful in America it would take them into a whole new league and the financial rewards would have a dramatic impact on the family's lifestyle: private education for the children, international holidays every year, a bigger house, a better car. It would all be possible.

Peter thought his wife would be elated, but unfortunately for him, his news was met with a rather mixed response. Peter's wife started off happy enough, but as he expanded on his ideas she became more and more negative about whether or not Peter's business would succeed in such a competitive market, and about the financial risks that would be involved in expanding in such a way. The tension with his wife had escalated into several rows and he couldn't understand what he had done wrong. He had expected his wife to be his biggest supporter.

When acquaintances or people of little significance in our lives challenge our ideas, it can be easy to brush off their opinions and tell yourself it doesn't matter what this person does or doesn't think, because they don't really matter to you. When someone you love is unable to support your goals it is often much more complicated and more of a challenge not to let their lack of belief compromise your own belief.

At first Peter couldn't see what there was not to love about where the business was headed, but slowly he began to understand things from his wife's perspective and he realised that it was understandable that she had mixed feelings. They would need to take a second mortgage on the house to fund the expansion and that placed the family's financial future at risk. If he was to expand into America it would mean regular travel and a lot of time away from the girls and he realised that all the trappings of success, the car, house, schools and so on weren't something his wife had ever expressed more than a passing desire for. To complicate things further, he remembered that his wife had once run a small business that she had decided to close down when the girls came along because it hadn't made enough money to be worth continuing with.

When someone else doesn't believe in you or your dreams, remember it's about them, not you.

Peter realised his wife's negativity had very little to do with her belief in him or the business and had everything to do with her need for security, her desire to have him around and her own sense of failure about her own business. He knew he had some work to do to get his wife to feel comfortable with the new direction, but he also knew that he didn't need to start doubting himself just because the person he loved most wasn't able to believe in his plans as much as he did.

When you believe in yourself, anything is possible. There's a line in the George Bernard Shaw play *Back to Methuselah*: 'You see things; and you say, "Why?" But I dream things that never were; and I say, "Why not?"' With a strong sense of self-belief, you too will be able to say 'why not?' to all your hopes, dreams and ideas.

It's hard to be unhappy when you believe your life is filled with possibility. The more you believe in yourself, the easier it will be for you to see the potential those possibilities hold and the more likely it is that they will become a reality in your life.

If your goal is to be the best you can be, nurturing your self-esteem and protecting your sense of self-worth will be valuable contributors to being able to say, 'I did my best and my best was good enough'. When you believe in yourself unconditionally, you will feel strong and confident in your attempts and, regardless of whether you succeed or fail, happy with who you are.

*If you believe in yourself,
anything and everything is possible.*

The **Fifth Key** is all about how you value yourself. Apply the *principle of belief*, rather than putting yourself down and undermining your self-belief, update your inner dialogue with new positive and encouraging messages. **Back yourself** and watch your self-belief grow.

Get Out of the Way

The Principle of Permission

One of the most powerful questions you can ask yourself is, 'How do I hold myself back?' While many people have some idea of what they want to do and who they want to be, one of the main reasons they are not already living that way is that on some level they are getting in their own way.

Life may present you with plenty of excuses, but the most common reason people don't have what they want is because they haven't given themselves permission to have it. Whether it is career success, romantic fulfilment, health, wealth or happiness, if you don't have it, it is usually because on some level you have consciously or subconsciously prevented it from becoming a reality in your life.

One of the most powerful questions you can ask yourself is, 'How do I hold myself back?' Once you know the answer you can get out of your way.

It may be that you accept your limiting beliefs, engage in self-sabotaging behaviour or simply never really try because you don't believe the kind of life you want could truly be yours. If you want to be the best you can be, one of the first things you need to do is give yourself permission to be that person.

If you don't truly believe that you deserve to be happy, or if on some level you are not giving yourself permission to truly *be* happy, then any happiness you experience will be fleeting and short term. You will only experience it on a surface level, not as something that provides deep and lasting contentment. Once you make the decision to be happy, you have to get out of your own way and do everything you can to maintain and sustain that state in your life.

*Being happy
is not a privilege—
it is something
everyone deserves.*

Being happy is not a privilege. Having a life full of all the things that matter most to you and in which you feel content is something everyone deserves, but so many people are waiting for it to happen or hoping someone else will give it to them. They either think that doing this or having that will make them happy, or that meeting Mr or Miss Right will guarantee a life of contentment. Happiness has to come from within, and is a state of being, not one of doing or having, and there isn't anything or anyone who can give it to you.

But sometimes people need to be reminded. I know I did. During the time when my life 'looked good on paper', I subconsciously knew I was letting myself down, and on a conscious level I felt guilty for not being satisfied with my 'lot'. My job was impressive and my boyfriend was a perfectly decent guy. For a long time I wondered what was wrong with me. Shouldn't I be happy with what I had, wouldn't other people be happy to be in my shoes, was I being ungrateful not to be more appreciative of my life?

The truth was, I wasn't ungrateful; I was unsatisfied, unfulfilled and unhappy. But before I could find my way out of this state, I needed to admit that my current state of affairs wasn't okay and I needed to give myself permission not only to make the changes I needed to make in my life, but also to acknowledge that I *wanted* to make these changes. I had to give myself permission to live my *best life*, not just any old life.

Once I gave myself permission to want *more*, nothing could hold me back. There was absolutely no way I could choose any path other than the one that would take me away from where I had been heading and towards the life I wanted to be living. When you stop apologising for the things you want, making them a reality in your life will seem the most natural thing in the world. I know I wouldn't be where I am today if I hadn't got out of my own way.

You have to give yourself permission to be happy. Nobody else can give it to you.

There is nothing wrong with wanting more: more fulfilment, better relationships, deeper happiness, better health or more laughter in your life. As long as you honour your values and focus on the things that matter most to you, there is no reason why you shouldn't have all that you want from life. Don't be afraid to make the words of Oliver Twist your new mantra: 'Please sir, I want some more!' Giving yourself permission to live your best possible life and fulfilling your potential is one of the surest ways to feel happy with who you are and all that you have.

There is nothing wrong with wanting more. There is no reason why you shouldn't get everything you want from life.

Give yourself permission to shine. I don't mean you need to be on a stage or doing something that involves the limelight, but you need to feel that *you* are the shining light in your life and that living your life is a vibrant and energised experience.

Our deepest fear is not that we are inadequate.
Our deepest fear is that we are powerful beyond measure.
It is our light, not our darkness that most frightens us.
We ask ourselves, Who am I to be brilliant, gorgeous,
talented, fabulous?
Actually, who are you not to be?
You are a child of God. Your playing small does not
serve the world.
There is nothing enlightened about shrinking
so that other people won't feel insecure around you.
We are all meant to shine, as children do.
We were born to make manifest the glory of God
that is within us.
It's not just in some of us; it's in everyone.
And as we let our own light shine, we unconsciously
give other people permission to do the same.
As we are liberated from our own fear,
our presence automatically liberates others.

Marianne Williamson
(from her book *A Return to Love*)

To be the best you can be, you need to challenge your assumptions and identify the existence of limiting beliefs. At first you may not even realise you have them. Many people accept their assumptions as fact and never think to confront their limits. Every time you find yourself thinking that you can't do something, ask yourself, 'Why not?' Each time you hear your inner voice telling you that something won't happen for you, tell yourself, 'You bet it will!' And when you find yourself holding back in case you fail, tell yourself that you know you will succeed.

*Challenge your assumptions
and identify your limiting beliefs.
Every time you find yourself thinking
that you can't do something,
ask yourself, 'Why not?'*

Emma was the receptionist in a busy recruitment consultancy. Although she was often hiding behind her fringe, her boss saw her potential and invited me to become her coach. One of the things Emma's boss had noticed was how warm and friendly she was to people who were coming in to the company for job interviews as sales agents, but how uncomfortable she seemed every time she had to speak to her colleagues or superiors.

It seemed that when Emma was worried about someone else, like a nervous interview candidate, she forgot about her lack of confidence and focused on putting the other person at ease. But the minute Emma became self-conscious for any reason, her shyness kicked in and she stuttered, stammered and generally clammed up. Emma's boss thought if she could build her confidence and allow more of the 'real Emma' to shine through, she would be a great asset to the company.

Emma and I began to explore the times when she felt the most confident, like when she was with family and old friends, and the situations in which she found her shyness the most overwhelming. One of occasions when she felt uncomfortable was coming up the following evening. Emma had to attend a work function. She would be expected to mingle and mix with colleagues, clients and candidates and she was dreading all the new people and all the small talk. The thing she tried to avoid most of all was finding herself in a situation where she would have to start a conversation with someone she didn't know, and at similar events in the past, Emma had usually found an excuse to leave early or a way to help out behind the scenes. As Richard Bach, the author of one of my favourite books, *Jonathan Livingston Seagull*, says, 'Argue for your limitations and sure enough they're yours'.

Emma had always accepted her assumptions as fact, and her limiting belief, that because she was shy she would never be able to enjoy meeting and mixing with new people, had defined many of her social experiences. I suggested that Emma consider a different scenario. What if she recognised her feelings of discomfort, acknowledged how nervous the thought of speaking to someone new made her feel, and then took a deep breath and went over and said hello anyway? Until this point it had never occurred to Emma that her shyness didn't have to get in her way, but what if she didn't have to overcome her shyness for things to change? What if she could recognise her feelings and then simply file them away under the heading 'unhelpful feelings' and carry on regardless? Emma was intrigued by this idea and agreed to give it a go.

Challenging your beliefs and assumptions is incredibly empowering. Sometimes, giving yourself permission to be the best you can be takes lots of practice and reinforcement, but other times it can be as simple as making the decision to see your potential in a new light and committing to this perspective from this point forward.

Emma always says that was the night that changed her life. She spent the whole evening mixing and mingling and although sick with nerves at first, she acknowledged her feelings, took a deep breath and went over to someone who was standing alone and introduced herself. Being able to do something she had previously found so intimidating made her feel invincible and like nothing could get in her way. It wasn't that her shyness had gone away, but the *power* she had been giving her shyness had gone away. Emma had let go of her limiting belief and given herself permission to shine.

One of the most common ways people limit themselves is with self-sabotage, actions or non-actions that actively compromise their chances of getting what they say they want. Self-sabotage can be direct, such as starting an argument in a job interview, skipping an exam or being unfaithful to your partner, or it can be more subtle, like allowing one drink to turn into four the night before the interview, not giving yourself enough time to revise before the exam or starting an argument because your relationship is going 'too well'.

So many people sabotage their own chances for happiness—don't be one of them.

Most people are guilty of sabotaging their own happiness to some degree by regularly doing things that compromise their goals or failing to do the things required in order to achieve them. If you think you may be guilty of self-sabotage, take an honest look at your counterproductive behaviours and unhelpful habits and ask yourself what is really going on. Either you don't really want what you say you want, or you are not giving yourself permission to go after the things you do want.

There are lots of different reasons why people sabotage their own efforts. It might be that you are so afraid of failure that you would rather defeat yourself before you start, or that you are terrified by the implications of success. It could be that you don't truly believe that you deserve the things you want or that you don't believe you will be able to get them, so you'd rather not try at all. When you think about the things you want from life, the easiest way to avoid self-sabotaging behaviour is to ask yourself, 'What habits do I need to put in place and what behaviours do I need to support if I am to make this desire a reality in my life?'

It's only when our actions are aligned with our words that we start to achieve our full potential. It's only when the things you say you want and the things you do to get what you want are consistent that you really have the chance to be the best you can be.

Sometimes the obstacles in your path can feel very real, such as the money you need to buy a house, the degree you need to get a job or the weight you need to lose. But these things don't have to stop you from getting what you want. Every time you find yourself saying 'but', what you are really doing is withholding permission from yourself. Each time you say 'but', what you really mean is, 'Here is my get-out clause, my excuse or my caveat that lets me off the hook from really going after what I want from life'. Although these factors may be genuine, it is up to you whether you see them as insurmountable obstacles or as hurdles you are ready to leap over. Only you can decide whether you will let them deter you from your goal or motivate you to find a way around them.

It is only when your actions and words are aligned that you can achieve your true potential.

When you give yourself permission to do, be and have all that you can in life, obstacles may still be present but they will no longer feel insurmountable. After all, we all know the story about someone who has made their way around one, if not many, hurdles to go on and achieve great success in their life. The challenges may still be there, but if you genuinely give yourself permission to achieve your potential, you won't let them get in your way.

Every time you say 'but', you are giving yourself a get-out clause.

Mark was feeling seriously unmotivated at work. He had what other people thought was a good job with one of the big investment banks, but he really wasn't enjoying it. He was confused and didn't know if the problem was his attitude or if the real answer to his happiness lay elsewhere.

Mark had joined the company five years ago, straight after completing his MBA. He had received two promotions during this time and the company had paid a big chunk of his MBA tuition fees as a sign-on bonus. Mark was worried that he sounded ungrateful when he talked about his frustrations with his job and one of the first things I did was reassure him that it was okay to want more. Just because his life looked good on paper, that didn't mean it couldn't be even better.

The last time Mark had felt truly inspired by the work he was doing was back in his mid-twenties, long before he had begun his MBA, when he was working at a small entrepreneurial company. Even though he'd been young, he was put in charge of creating a whole new division for this business and he had loved it. He had always thought he wanted to be an entrepreneur and this exciting experience only confirmed this desire for him.

Although Mark was excited about the thought of becoming a 'real' entrepreneur, he also found the idea a little daunting. He had an idea for a new product and he realised the first thing he would need was some money to make his plan a reality. Although he had some savings he certainly didn't have enough money to get his plan off the ground. That was where he hit his first obstacle: how to get a bank or institution to lend money to someone as young and comparatively inexperienced as him.

Mark decided the best thing to do would be to get more qualified, so he enrolled in an MBA. He told himself that once he had more business knowledge he would be a better entrepreneur and people would be more likely to back him in his endeavours. That was fifteen years ago.

Mark completed his MBA and accumulated the huge debt that went with it. He figured he had better get his loan paid off before he started focusing on his business ideas, so he got a job with a big bank. Then he met his future wife and they decided to buy a house together. Mark saw the savings he had managed to put aside for his business become part of the deposit on the house but he comforted himself with the idea that when his home grew in value he would have equity against it to secure his loan. Then Mark's wife fell pregnant. He figured he had better pay as much off the house as he could before it was time to start thinking about school fees. And so on it went until fifteen years had passed with Mark no closer to his entrepreneurial dreams.

No wonder Mark was unhappy. Rather than back himself, he had subconsciously found obstacle after obstacle to prevent him from going after his dream. Once Mark realised what had been going on, he was able to look at his dream of becoming an entrepreneur in a more honest light. He realised that although he had started out doubting his own abilities, which may have been the reason he put the first obstacle in his path, he had since come to enjoy the security and comfort that his corporate life had provided. Slowly, over time, Mark had started to value his corporate life. Although he had never given himself permission to pursue his entrepreneurial dream, he was now clinging to that fantasy rather than giving himself permission to enjoy his corporate life for all that it had to offer.

There is nothing wrong with deciding that you don't want something, but if you do want it, go out and get it!

There is nothing wrong with consciously choosing not to pursue a particular path and it's natural to experience conflict when considering the impact of making a certain change. Very few things in life are black and white, and taking the time to ensure the path you are choosing is the right one for you is always worthwhile, but there is a big difference between not knowing whether you want something and not permitting yourself to pursue the things you do want.

Any time you can think of something you want from life, and you can't see yourself being clearly on track to having it, look at how you might be holding yourself back and what you need to do to get out of your own way. This can be challenging but don't be afraid of what you might find. It is never pleasant to uncover a limiting belief, realise what you had assumed to be fact was just an obstacle *you* placed in your path, or recognise you have been engaging in a pattern of self-sabotaging behaviour. But once you have discovered the ways in which you have relinquished permission, you are free to develop new thoughts, habits and behaviours that support the life you do want to have.

When you stop holding yourself back and give yourself permission to truly be the best you can be, lifelong happiness will come naturally to you.

*Just because there is an obstacle
in your path, that doesn't mean
you have to get off the road.*

The **Sixth Key** is all about allowing yourself to get the most out of life. Every time you find yourself thinking about your future, but following that thought with a 'but' or 'if only', remember that you are the one getting in your own way. Apply the *principle of permission*; instead of engaging in excuses for why your life isn't all that it could be, **get out of the way** and create your life as you want it to be.

Be Grateful

The Principle of Abundance

Worrying about money is one of the biggest causes of unhappiness for so many people. It is not money itself that is the problem, but the feelings people have about it. It has very little to do with how much or how little you have and everything to do with your perspective on the wealth and abundance in your life.

How do you feel when you think about money? Regardless of your financial circumstances, do you focus on all that you *don't* have: a bigger house, a new kitchen, a faster car, designer clothes or more shoes?

*Worrying about money is
one of the biggest causes of
unhappiness, but no amount
of money can make you happy
unless you change the
way you feel about it.*

If you want to be truly happy with your life, rather than focusing your energy on what you don't have, shift your attention to all that you do have. Focus on feeling gratitude for the wealth and abundance that is already in your life.

At first this advice may seem to contradict what you see as the role of a coach; after all, I've just been talking about the importance of giving yourself permission to do, be and *have* all that you can in life. And it's true: if there is something you would like to have in life and you are willing to do what it takes to get it, then you should definitely go after it. But just because there are

things you desire, that doesn't mean you can't enjoy the
life you already have.

*Just because there are things
you still want, that doesn't mean
you can't feel gratitude for all the
wealth and abundance
already in your life.*

A poverty mentality is a serious affliction and it
appears to be reaching epidemic proportions. In the
world we live in today, there are millions of people
living in genuine poverty, but unless you work with the
poor and underprivileged it is most likely the people
you mix with in your day-to-day life will be firmly of
'comfortable' status. Sure, for some, things might not be
perfect. They might have had to tighten their belts in
the wake of recent economic upheavals or perhaps they
don't have all the luxuries in their life that they would

like. Of course, some people are genuinely struggling, but the people I hear complaining about not having enough money usually have everything they really need.

Having a poverty mentality leaves you focusing on all the things you don't have, when in reality you probably already have everything you need.

My best friend calls these people the 'avocado poor'; they might not have everything they want, but they are happy to buy gourmet fresh fruit and vegetables, out of season, and are probably paying for the 'ready ripe' variety while they're at it. People with a poverty mentality complain about not being able to afford a home extension, or to send their children to the right private school or buy the latest must-have gadget, all the while having more than enough food on the table, a roof over their head, clothes in their wardrobe and, in many cases, money in the bank.

The level of abundance in the majority of people's lives means they shouldn't have anything to complain about but unfortunately, in the consumption-crazy times we live in, it seems there are a lot of affluent people convinced they don't have enough.

Caroline was one of those people who was never happy with what she had; she always wanted more. Caroline liked to 'keep up with the Joneses'. If a friend had a new outfit, she wanted a new outfit. When one of her friends remodelled their kitchen Caroline immediately started talking about how much she hated her kitchen, how she really needed to have a new one installed. When one of Caroline's closest friends moved to a bigger house, one with a swimming pool, sure enough, Caroline declared her house so small it was 'practically an embarrassment'.

Caroline had a serious poverty mentality. She saw everything in her life from the point of view of what she didn't have. She was *always* talking about what she didn't have. What clothes she wished she could buy. How she was forced to go on a three-star holiday when some of her friends could afford five-star. How she was embarrassed about her house but that she and her husband were 'too poor' to buy a bigger one. Not only did she resent the absence of these things in her life, but her attitude prevented her from being able to enjoy and appreciate the things she did have.

I told Caroline she was one of the richest poor people I knew. She laughed indignantly at first and declared that she wasn't rich at all. I pressed on and reminded her that, given how poor she was always saying she was, she sure had a lot of good things in her life. I started to make a list. Although she didn't have a swimming pool, she certainly wasn't living under a bridge. She had a perfectly decent house in a perfectly decent suburb. She had been on two holidays in the last year and although she hadn't stayed at the Four Seasons, she had enjoyed her time in a lovely family resort. On top of this, she had a good relationship with her husband, two happy, healthy children, some money saved for retirement and little else to complain about.

Faced with the facts, Caroline had to concede that she wasn't poor. It was just that there were so many things she wanted, but didn't have, that she felt she was missing out all the time.

Even if there are things you desire, that doesn't mean you can't enjoy the things you already have. These are not mutually exclusive events. Enjoying the roof you have over your head doesn't stop you from planning to buy a bigger house. Enjoying your cheap and cheerful holiday doesn't prevent you from saving up for something a bit more luxurious next time. Being grateful for all that you *already* have in life won't hold you back from getting more. It will just mean that you enjoy the life you do have so much more.

Caroline was missing out, but not on the things she thought. The majority of the things she wanted were just material possessions. What she was missing out on was the chance to enjoy and appreciate all the lovely things she did have in her life. By constantly pining for something more and constantly coveting what her friends had, Caroline was wasting the opportunity to enjoy all the things she did have: the home she lived in and the holidays she went on, not to mention the fact that she would probably get to enjoy her friend's pool in the summer without the responsibility of keeping it clean and free of leaves.

The problem with a poverty mentality is that it starts out focused on financial poverty: thinking you don't have enough money, thinking you don't have enough things. But if you are in the habit of thinking about what you *don't have* rather than recognising the abundance in your life, you will soon find yourself experiencing a state of emotional or spiritual poverty too, where you can't enjoy the simple pleasures in life without thinking about what you are going without.

One of the biggest challenges Caroline was experiencing was understanding the difference between *want* and *need*. She thought she *needed* all of those things, the clothes, the kitchen, the holidays and bigger house, and that without them she couldn't be happy, but the truth was, she simply wanted them. The loss of clarity between want and need is a big problem in our media-saturated lives. The entire advertising industry exists to convince us our lives would be better if we did this and feel much happier if we bought that.

The ancient Greek philosopher Epictetus said, 'Wealth consists not in having great possessions, but in having few wants'. The more you can recognise the existing abundance in your life and realise how little difference purchases and acquisitions will really make, the happier you will be.

*When you understand
the difference between
want and need, you will
finally realise how
rich your life really is.*

Do you really need a bigger house? Probably not.
A new TV? Not while the old one is still working and
even then, I'm sure you could live without one for a
while. Do you need new clothes, new shoes? Not unless
there are holes in the ones you are wearing.

All you really need is a roof over your head, some
food to eat, clothes to cover your body and some warm
and caring relationships in your life. Sadly, there are
some people in our society and millions throughout
the world who don't have even their most basic needs
met, but this is exactly my point. There is a huge
difference between being in poverty and having a
poverty mentality.

In our society today most people have their basic needs so well and truly met that they are able to completely take them for granted. The energy they might have once needed to apply to meeting their needs is now applied to pursuing their wants. That your happiness should not be dependent on having your *wants* met seems for many to have been lost in translation.

Getting clear on the difference between your wants and needs is one of the most liberating things you can do. Once you realise you probably already have everything you *need*, you are free to relax and enjoy some of the extra things in your life for what they really are … trimmings.

*There is nothing wrong
with enjoying life's luxuries
as long as your happiness
isn't contingent on them.*

Don't worry; I am not going to suggest you need to live an austere or monastic life in order to be happy. I am the first person to put my hand up and say I enjoy lovely things. Personally, I'm a big fan of life's little luxuries and, for that matter, many of life's bigger luxuries too, but my happiness is not contingent on having them in my life.

Before I became a coach I worked as an independent management consultant in the high-powered world of investment banking. It was highly lucrative work and I had nobody's financial needs to consider but my own. My work was challenging, demanding and high-pressured, and I was rewarded well for it. I took taxis everywhere, thought nothing about popping out for a new pair of designer shoes at lunchtime or flying somewhere warm for the weekend. And five-star restaurants, well they were where I went, simply because I had to eat.

When I decided it was time for a career change I knew I would have to make significant changes to my lifestyle. Of course I would still be living a great life, but I would be building a coaching practice from scratch, in a new city where I had very few contacts and no professional history to draw on. A lot of the luxuries that I had previously taken for granted would now need to become occasional or even rare pleasures.

Several of my friends wondered how I would cope with this shift in my lifestyle and spending habits, and one even questioned whether I should go ahead with my plans at all. But I was undeterred. I was confident that not only would I continue to enjoy my life, but I would probably enjoy it even more as I would be doing work I really loved and was passionate about … I just might not be doing it in designer shoes!

In reality, the transition was easy for me. I knew the trade-off was well and truly worth it and recognised that all the luxuries I had enjoyed were how I had decorated my life, not how I defined it. Whether I am wearing designer shoes from Italy or walking around in my rubber Havaianas has no bearing on my happiness at all. Of course, over time as my business grew and I succeeded at many of the goals I had set myself, I was able to once again splurge on some of my favourite treats. While I enjoy the pleasures money can buy, it is not what makes me happy. I'm happy in who I am and I know the life I lead is a rich and rewarding one, regardless of what I'm wearing on my feet!

Most of the things you find yourself wanting will have little or no bearing on the happiness in your life.

So many of the things people want in their lives bear little or no relation to the things that will make them happy. They see material possessions as a way of creating or defining happiness rather than as a way of accessorising an already happy and fulfilling life.

If you want to know what *things* will make you happy, you need to go back and review your values. Unless there were specific material possessions that made it onto your list of the things that matter most in your life, you can't expect having them to have more than a cursory effect on your long-term happiness. Sure, you might get a rush of exhilaration when you buy them, but it will only be a short-term thrill and will have little or no impact on your long-term happiness.

If you want to experience sustained happiness in your life, you need to be continuously appreciative of the wealth and abundance in your life. The quickest way to get an abundance mindset is to express your thanks for all that you have, to think about all the things you are grateful for and to acknowledge this with an expression of gratitude. Some people may like to offer a prayer of thanks, but if that's not your style acknowledging your gratitude to yourself can be just as powerful.

Find a way to express your gratitude for the wealth and abundance in your life.

Many people are so caught up in a poverty mentality or a desire to have more that they find it very difficult to recognise the abundance already in their life. Not only do they miss out on the joy expressing gratitude brings into your life, but by focusing on all that they don't have, they exist in a state of scarcity where nothing is ever enough and so are constantly experiencing frustration, anxiety and resentment instead of joy, happiness and contentment.

Adam was an investment banker. I know I said I was doing well when I worked in that environment, but Adam was a *serious* high flyer and he was earning well over a million dollars a year by the time he was thirty. The problem was, ten years and many millions later, Adam wasn't happy. He found his work exhausting and he was tired of being under constant pressure from working on big deals. Adam felt completely trapped in his wealth and now that he was thinking about quitting work and changing careers, all he could think about was losing all his money.

Initially Adam wanted things to change without having to make any changes. He was tired of the long hours and high pressure of the job that he had, but was worried about earning any less than he was used to. To any observer it would appear that Adam's hard work had placed him in the most fortunate position. His home was worth several million dollars and he owned it outright. He had an investment portfolio that performed well each year and he had money in the bank. Plenty of people would have been planning their retirement if their financial position was as robust as Adam's, but not him. Adam had a scarcity mentality and he was worried about 'losing it all'.

Focusing on scarcity will only create more of the same.

The first shift of perspective that Adam needed was to realise that to change jobs or even to take some time out from work wasn't going to take away all that he had worked for. Even if he never found another job, which, given his skills and experience, was highly unlikely, it wasn't like his house could be repossessed; he didn't have a mortgage on it!

I asked Adam how much money he thought he needed to live on each month but he didn't know the answer. I clarified my question. I wasn't asking him to tell me his monthly budget or spending plan. Just what he though he actually *needed* every month.

When Adam worked out what he would need to cover his basic needs—food, petrol for the car, money for gas, electricity and other bills and a small amount of spending money for incidentals—it came to a little over a thousand dollars a month.

Then I asked Adam what he thought his net worth needed to be before he felt secure and confident enough to make a move. His answer was astonishing. Despite having a home that was fully paid for and no dependants relying on him for security, Adam felt he needed twenty million dollars before he would feel truly confident in his financial future.

Once I composed myself I challenged Adam on his assessment. How many times over would his basic needs have to be met before he felt confident to make a change? Adam tried to make an excuse. Basic needs weren't all he would need; he still wanted to be able to live a comfortable life. But Adam wasn't an extravagant man and his day-to-day expenses would have to go up astronomically to even put a dent in the nest egg he felt he had to have.

Coming from his banking background, Adam was good with numbers and he could quickly see how extreme his assessment had been. He realised he had been living with a scarcity mentality, worrying about his money running out, rather than enjoying the abundance of it in his life. Once Adam shifted his perspective, he was able to make a more sensible plan, one that would provide him with the security he needed, but also give him the confidence to make the move he craved.

Before you say that's crazy, that would never happen to me, ask yourself, 'What if the numbers on the table were smaller?' How much money do you think you need to have before you have enough? How big does your nest egg need to be before you feel free to pursue your dreams? And how much would you be willing to risk if it meant living a happier and more fulfilling life?

Throughout my work I've had a similar conversation to the one I had with Adam with many other people. The numbers are usually smaller, but all too often the fears are just the same. People are afraid to give up or risk even a small amount of money to achieve the changes they want in their life, more freedom, better balance or simply a change of scene, because money or scarcity of it is such a defining force in their lives.

Although Adam was concerned about risking his financial security, he was also concerned about risking the status that came with his level of wealth. All too often, people allow money to be the only measure of success in their lives. Rather than looking at whether they are happy, healthy, surrounded by loved ones and living with integrity, they measure their worth strictly in dollars and cents.

Sometimes you have to risk or give up some of your financial wealth to have a richer life.

You will have a much better understanding of the true wealth in your life when you think about all the things you have to be grateful for: your health, loving relationships, a variety of experiences, the quality of the food you eat, the environment and home you live in and the fundamental safety and security of your life. Just because each of these may not be perfect or there may still be room for improvement, that doesn't mean that you can't express gratitude for your life as it is.

The only way to get an understanding of the true wealth in your life is to acknowledge all the things you have to be grateful for.

The **Seventh Key** is all about recognising how rich your life really is. Begin each day by focusing on the things for which you are grateful. Apply the *principle of abundance*; any time you find yourself focusing on 'lack of' or deficiency in your life, recall this list, re-establish your awareness of the abundance in your life and **be grateful** for all that you have.

Give All You Can

The Principle of Generosity

If you want happiness to flow through your life, being generous is like turning on the tap. The more we can give, the more we will receive, whether it is time, money, love or attention.

Many people think they are generous, but all they are considering are the decisions they make with their wallets: the money they spend and the price tags on the gifts they buy. But being generous is about so much more than that. Generosity can be a little gesture, like feeding someone's parking meter or handing someone the right change for their ticket when they get on the bus. It might be treating a friend to lunch for no reason other than 'just because', or taking the time to really listen to an elderly relative telling you their favourite story *again*. Sometimes being generous is as simple as giving someone the benefit of the doubt and trusting that however things may feel right now, like you, they are probably just doing the best they can.

Being generous is not just about the decisions you make with your wallet. Being generous with your time and energy is just as important.

One of the easiest ways to practise generosity, to borrow from the author Richard Carlson, is, 'Don't Sweat the Small Stuff'. So many people view their relationships as transactional affairs, keeping a mental ledger of who paid for coffee, who returned the call, who gave the more expensive gift, who bought the groceries, who booked the restaurant and so on.

Be generous with your friends and loved ones. Don't worry if on this occasion you gave them a little more than they gave you. If your relationship, romantic, platonic or familial, is filled with love and affection, you are bound to receive in return as much as you give.

If you stop worrying about these small details and start to realise that if your relationship is a good one things will balance out over time, you will be much happier. Equality in any relationship doesn't have to be an exact science. One person may contribute more financially, while another contributes in other ways. You may be engaged in a friendship where you are the one who always picks up the phone, but your friend regularly picks up the bill. I know I have one particular friend who almost never calls, but if ever I am going through a tough time she is the first to send flowers, a card or some other 'I'm thinking of you' gift. Her thoughtfulness at the times that really matter more than makes up for the fact that I am the one who initiates our communication. It may be that your partner covers most of the household outgoings, but you do all of the organising and home administration, or perhaps you arrange for all the family gifts at Christmas time but your partner does all the cooking.

If you are generous in your relationships you will receive as much as you give.

If you really feel that you can't stop keeping tabs on who is doing what in the relationship, who bought the last coffee, who made the last call, who booked the restaurant, who paid the taxi driver, then perhaps you need to reconsider the values you hold around relationships or the people with whom you choose to have relationships.

Often we can find ourselves existing in our own little bubble, thinking that the only life experience is our life experience and the only circumstances that matter are our own. The truth is that one of the fastest ways to increase the level of happiness in your own life is to recognise how fortunate you are and to be generous to those less fortunate than yourself. This might be by committing a regular financial contribution to a cause you believe in, or it could be that you volunteer your time to an organisation that could really use your helping hand.

Being generous to those less fortunate than you is not just about contributing time or money. It also means not judging someone on their appearance, education, accent or experiences. Everyone is on a different journey and each person has a different story to tell. Before you judge, remember that the other person may not have had the advantages you have had or, even if they have, they may have chosen to interpret or apply them in a different way than you.

Everyone has a different journey in life. Don't judge someone else for theirs.

When you judge someone what you are really trying to do is find a way of saying 'I'm better than you', even if it is a silent, internal conversation. You gain nothing of any value by thinking you are better than someone else—only a momentary ego boost, a false sense of pride or support for a racial, moral or social stereotype, which are all best avoided.

Each time you say, 'I don't mean to judge but ...', that is exactly what you are doing, marking your perspective as superior and the other person's as being in some way, shape or form inferior to your own.

One of the most insightful quotes regarding judgement is from Voltaire, who said, 'Judge a person by their questions, rather than their answers'. In other words, take a minute to understand their perspective, their values and the reasons why they might be making the choices that they are making.

Take parenting for example. There are hundreds of different views and every parent is just trying to work out what is right for them and their child. Everyone has a different view. Subjects like feeding, sleeping, disciplining and schooling are currently being hotly debated all over the western world. But is there really one right answer? Of course not. The only right answer is the one that meets the needs and honours the values of each individual family. Does it matter whether your child sleeps in bed with you or in their own cot? Not as long as it is within the safety guidelines and everybody is getting *some* sleep. Does it matter when your child feeds or for how long? Not as long as the child is getting all the nutrition they need. Should you use a naughty step, a time out or direct punishment? Does it really matter as long as the behaviour of the child in question improves? Is public school better than private in the long term? I am sure you can round up a team of people to debate the merits of each.

Before passing judgement
on someone's choices,
stop and look at the questions
they were trying to answer.

For these and most other questions in life, there usually isn't one right answer, just the right answer for the people involved. Before you find yourself getting caught judging someone else's choice because it is different from your own, ask yourself what they are trying to achieve. With this parenting example, I am sure each parent involved would tell you they are just trying to do what is best for their child. Regardless of the individual response, the question remains the same: What is right for my child? What is best for my family? It is only the answers that change.

Next time you find yourself drawn towards judging someone and the choices they have made, first consider the questions they are trying to answer and the values they are aiming to honour. You may find you have a different opinion or that in the same situation you would have made a different choice, but an opinion is not a judgement. It is only a judgement when you feel you are superior because of the opinion you hold.

I firmly believe most people are doing their best, most of the time. Not everyone and not all of the time, but the majority of people the majority of the time, and one of the simplest acts of generosity you can offer someone is to make this assumption. Life is full of potentially frustrating situations. You might be annoyed with your partner, friend or family member who is making a choice you don't agree with. You might be annoyed with the person in customer service because they can't answer your question, or with a member of your team for not getting a piece of work in on time. Each time an irritating situation arises, before you let it really wind you up, take a deep breath and make the assumption that the person in question is just trying to do their best. When you take this approach, not only will you feel the majority of your tension or frustration dissipate almost immediately, but you will find, if you can give the other person the benefit of the doubt, your generosity will be repaid by a shift in the way they respond to you and a reduction in negativity all round.

Most people are doing their best, most of the time.

If you want to be the best you can be, don't judge anyone. Not even yourself. Paula is one of the hardest-working, most committed people I know. She is a loving and supportive wife, a brilliant mother to two young children and very successful at her part-time job in the media. Paula is on the committee at her children's school, always buys local and recycles or composts everything she can. She remembers people's birthdays, babysits her brother's children and regularly visits her Gran. Paula would be an example to anyone who is trying to be the best they can be, but she just can't see it for herself.

The problem is, Paula is so generous with her time, her love and her patience with everyone except for herself. Any time I see Paula she is always able to give me a list of the million and one tiny little ways she has failed since we last spoke. Perhaps she got annoyed with one of her kids for not doing as she asked. Maybe she screened a call from her mum because she was making a cup of tea or perhaps she made a typo on a proposal for a client at work. Paula is always criticising herself for something.

If only she was as kind to herself as she is to others. I asked Paula what she would say to a friend who was juggling as many things as she was and she admitted she would think they were pretty amazing. She would also wonder how they could keep all their balls in the air without letting any drop and if something minor did drop, it wouldn't be for any other reason than because 'these things happen'.

Paula needed to ease up on herself and offer herself the same generosity she would to any of her friends. There is a big difference between being perfect, a wholly impossible goal, and being the best you can be. When you are being the best you can be, you know that as long as you've given your best, your best will always be good enough. And if some days your best is a little average, well that is just a part of being human.

If you want to be the best you can be, don't judge anyone. Not even yourself.

I asked Paula to think of one of her children's star charts. If she created a star chart for herself even she had to admit it would be covered in stars!

Remember to afford yourself
the same generosity
you give to others.

To be generous also means being kind and patient with yourself. Are you constantly criticising yourself, beating yourself up for not achieving this or failing to do that? Or do you encourage yourself, providing yourself with the positive reinforcement you need to take whatever is the next step? If you want to encourage a child to do something, you will speak to them in a kind and patient way. If you want to get the best out of yourself you need to take the same approach.

One of the most significant ways you can be generous is with your time and energy. Unfortunately, in the hustle-bustle world we live in it is this simple form of generosity that is most commonly forgotten. One of the greatest gifts you can give someone is attention. *Really* listen to them: not just hearing the words they are saying, but being present to *what* they are saying and why they are saying it.

When you offer someone quality listening, you don't interrupt, having decided what you are going to ask next before they have finished speaking; you don't say 'I know what you mean' or try to hurry them up by finishing their sentence for them; and you definitely don't check your emails, send a text or read the newspaper while they are speaking.

The harder it is to offer someone quality listening, the more important it is that you give it to them. When you are speaking with the elderly they can sometimes ramble or repeat themselves, but given the journey that they have been on in their life, surely they have earned a few minutes of your time. Give it to them. This simple act of generosity will mean the world to them.

The same goes for young children. They stutter and stumble, can't quite get the words out or get lost in their imagination mid sentence. Get down to their eye level and give them one hundred per cent of your attention. Be patient and kind. This will help them to focus and get clear about what they are really trying to say, and it will do wonders for their budding confidence and self-esteem.

Be generous with your time and energy. The harder it is to give, the more the other person deserves it.

Of course, the other people who really do deserve the gift of your attention are the people you love most in the world: husbands, wives, partners, parents and children. The people who matter most often get rushed along and receive the worst of our attention as they get lost in our desire to multi-task, complete our chores or simply catch up on our favourite show on TV. When you are truly generous, you give the people you love the best of yourself and you prioritise them above all others.

*Give the people you love the
best of yourself, not the worst.*

Sam really enjoyed his work. He had started out as
a dentist and was now a partner in a group of dental
practices throughout the city. Sam was ambitious. As
well as running his practices he was the national
president of his professional association and when he
wasn't thinking about teeth, he was working to reduce
his golf handicap. To Sam, there never seemed to be
enough hours in the day. He was always rushing here and
there, into this meeting, treating that patient, taking this
telephone call, writing that report. He liked to keep fit, so
when he got up in the morning he always went for a run
and his evenings were often spent writing for professional
publications and attending business functions.

Sam's professional colleagues admired him for all he
had achieved and his friends thought he had it all. From
the outside he did. Until the day his wife told him she
was filing for divorce. Sam was completely blindsided.

He had thought his wife was happy. They lived in a beautiful home, there was no shortage of money and they took regular holidays to luxury destinations. They had two teenage boys who were doing well at school and their life was the envy of all their peers.

The problem was, his wife didn't want to be the object of someone's envy; she wanted to be the recipient of her husband's attention. Although she enjoyed the trappings of Sam's success, the house, cars and holidays were never things she had craved and she would happily have given it all up just to get back the Sam she had married. She had known he was ambitious and in the beginning she had been very supportive, but in the last few years she had begun to resent the business and the way it consumed Sam's time.

With all the things going on in Sam's life he had very little time for his family. His wife had been trying to discuss this with him for months, but every time she brought it up, he said he was 'too busy to get into it right now'. He regularly cancelled their dinner plans on account of having to work late and he never turned up to functions at the boys' school.

Sam hadn't meant to be a negligent husband or father. He loved his wife and sons dearly, but he had been so busy focusing on his own goals and the things he wanted to do with his time that he never had anything left for them. He had taken the people he loved the most for granted, subconsciously thinking that they would always be there.

Providing people with quality attention, being patient and kind and allowing them the time they deserve is one of the best ways we can demonstrate to the people we love how much we really value them. In the modern world, time is one of our scarcest resources and by giving of our time we show our love in far greater ways than any gift ever could.

Fortunately for Sam his wife's mind wasn't fully made up. He'd never thought he was the 'counselling type' but he was willing to do anything if it meant saving his marriage. In time, with the help of their marriage therapist, Sam was able to see that all the luxury in the world didn't mean a thing if he didn't give his wife and sons the attention they deserved. Sam could see that he had been measuring his success in life in terms of what he could earn, rather than what he could give, and while he didn't have to give up everything he enjoyed, he would need to be much more generous towards his loved ones if his marriage was to get a second chance.

Sam, like so many people, was so caught up in his own goals, his own dreams and his own desire for success that he was neglecting the people who mattered most. He was measuring his success by the money he earned and his generosity by the gifts he could buy and the lifestyle he could provide.

*Recognise how much
you have to give.*

The **Eighth Key** is about so much more than money. It means being generous with both your time and your energy, being patient and kind with yourself and others, and avoiding judgement. Apply the *principle of generosity*; make the commitment to **give all you can**, whenever you can.

To laugh often and much;
to win the respect of intelligent people
and the affection of children;
to earn the appreciation of honest critics
and to endure the betrayal of false friends;
to appreciate beauty; to find the best in others;
to leave the world a bit better,
whether by a healthy child, a garden patch,
or a redeemed social condition;
to know even one life has breathed easier
because you have lived.
This is to have succeeded.

Ralph Waldo Emerson

Keep It Up

The Principle of Commitment

For most people, being happy isn't something that just happens. First, they have to make the choice to be happy, and then they must act on that choice consistently and continuously throughout their life. Deciding to be happy can cause a fundamental shift in your perspective, but it is acting on that decision that will have a lasting and sustainable impact on your life. Happiness is a state of *being*, but for most people a certain amount of *doing* is required to get and keep you there.

Although happiness is a state of being, it usually still requires some doing if it is to be lasting in your life.

Every single day you are faced with a series of the most ordinary choices. When to get up, what to have for breakfast, whether or not to exercise, coffee versus tea, how to handle a difficult colleague at work, whether to call your mother, what to have for dinner, whether your dinner will go better with a glass of wine, what to watch on TV and when to go to bed. Even if you are not consciously aware of it, you are constantly making decisions all through the day. The choices you make can either support your desire for happiness or undermine it.

Start the day fresh, eat well, exercise, be respectful of your colleagues, enjoy a drink in moderation, watch only a small amount of TV and go to bed before you are exhausted. These choices are all part of the prescription for feeling good about your life, but at any point in your day you could just as easily make the alternative choice. Sleep in, skip breakfast, self-medicate with coffee, run out of time to exercise, snap at your colleagues, drown your sorrows and fall into bed exhausted … hardly a prescription for a happy day. The point I am making is that you don't just have to make the right decisions once; you need to keep making them each and every day (or at least the majority of the time) if you expect happiness to be the natural state in your life.

Commit to being happy and make the choices that will support your commitment.

Just as this is true for the little decisions you make, it's equally important for the big decisions in your life. You need to be both active and proactive if you want to feel happy about your life. You need to not only be active in continually doing the things that contribute to your short-term, day-to-day happiness, but also work towards making your longer-term plans a reality in your life.

A fulfilling and meaningful life isn't something that just happens. It's something you need to create. Once you have made this a reality in your life, you can't take it for granted. Your core values might not change throughout your life, but the expression of those values will need to evolve as your life moves through its various stages.

You have to actively nurture the happiness and fulfilment in your life and continue to encourage yourself to grow and develop within it.

Don't take your happiness for granted. Be proactive about maintaining and sustaining it in your life.

Tania had always thought of herself as a happy person. She had been married for twenty-five years and while her marriage was not perfect, she considered it to be one of the 'good ones' and was happy to say she still found her husband attractive after all these years. She was fit and healthy. She had two sons, the youngest of whom had just headed overseas for a 'gap' year before starting university.

Before her boys were born, Tania had worked as an account director in a large public relations consultancy. It was a demanding and challenging job. She worked long hours and was paid well for it. Tania went back to work part time after her first son was born, but she didn't enjoy it nearly as much. At first she had more work than she could sensibly manage in the available time, and after six months of taking work home every single night, she spoke to her boss and scaled her responsibilities right back. The problem then was that she no longer found the work rewarding. When her second son came along, Tania decided to leave her job altogether and concentrate on parenting.

It had been a tough decision to make. She had always seen herself as a 'career woman' and quitting work to be a full-time mum was the last thing she had thought she would want to do. But in its current form, work hadn't been working, and Tania knew something needed to change. She thought she could trial this new life for six to twelve months and if she still wasn't happy she would have to look at other alternatives.

To Tania's delight, she loved her new role. After years of trying to keep both her bosses and her clients happy, she loved thinking about school lunches and play dates and enjoyed putting her creative mind to use, coming up with fun activities for the boys. She still took on the occasional PR consulting role, but it was always on a short-term basis and usually for small business, where the pressure and ego from her previous life were thankfully absent. Tania loved that she still got the chance to 'keep the cogs turning' while being active and present in her sons' lives and she felt very fulfilled and happy in her life.

At least she did until recently. Tania had been mindful of the 'empty nest' when her boys went to university and she had filled her diary with committee meetings, lunches with friends and a regular game of tennis, but she still felt really flat. At first she though she was just missing her youngest and it was true, she was missing her 'baby boy', but there was more to it than that.

Tania realised that the life that had been working so well for her wasn't fitting the bill anymore. Now that both of her boys had left home, she knew she would have to make some changes in her life, to get back her sense of fulfilment and satisfaction. She was pretty sure she wouldn't enjoy going back into corporate life, but she also thought the bits and bobs of work she had been doing weren't enough. She thought that starting her own small PR consultancy might give her the chance to use her brain a bit more, without having to give up the freedom and sense of balance in her life. Knowing that she at least knew *what* needed to change, Tania felt better than she had done in weeks and she was sure that once she put some of her ideas into action, she would have her mojo back in no time.

One of the reasons Tania was able to identify the changes she needed to make *before* she became unhappy was that she recognised the need to be proactive about maintaining happiness in her life. Tania knew she couldn't sit back and wait for her sense of fulfilment to return. She knew the answer was to go out and seek fulfilment and that if the first thing she tried didn't work, she would keep trying until she found something that did work.

Making the decision to be the best you can be can have a profound effect on your life. You become liberated from ideals of perfection and are able to move through life more confidently and with a greater sense of ease. But not all the immediate effects of this life-transforming decision may feel positive. One of the most challenging things people sometimes experience is a sense of isolation or distance from some of the people in their life. Most people are fine with *fine* and plenty of people are okay with *okay*. Not everyone wants to do what it takes to live their best life. They may whinge or complain about the life they have, but they really aren't prepared to do anything about changing it. If you want to be happy and fulfilled in life, it will take a little effort, and a lot of commitment to be continually making that effort.

Sometimes, when you make the commitment to being your best, other people can find it confronting. If some of the people in your life are content with their discontent or not discontented enough to act on it, it can create tension or even conflict. Although ego is probably the last thing that is motivating you to make changes in your life, people who are less confident or secure in their choices may accuse you of thinking that you're better than everyone else. Others may accuse you of being critical of their lives, when actually all you are focusing on is your own life.

*Most people are fine with fine
and okay with okay.
If you want to be the best you
can be, make sure you're not.*

I always remind my clients that it can be lonely at the top. When you are accepting of average, there are millions of people around you with that same low benchmark for the quality of their lives. As soon as you give yourself permission to be the best you can be and to live up to your potential, the pool of people who think the same way becomes smaller, and at first it can seem much, much smaller.

It can be uncomfortable but this is when your commitment really matters. The only person you are accountable to is you and the only person whose happiness you are responsible for is yours. Don't let anyone else hold you back from happiness or keep you from being the best you can be.

When you decide to be the best you can be, don't be surprised if the circle of people you want to spend your time with becomes smaller.

The majority of the time any negativity you experience from other people will be subtle and they possibly won't even realise they are being negative. If you notice someone in your circle behaving differently towards you as you embark upon the changes you need to make to be happy in your life, it's important to remember, it's not about you … it's about them. Perhaps they are feeling unsettled by the changes you are making, concerned by the shift in the status quo, self-conscious about the choices they have made in their own life or worried that you won't see *them* in the same light. Maybe they are uncomfortable about their own weight problem, wishing they could quit smoking, saddened by the state of their own unhappy marriage or wishing they had the courage to quit the job they hate. Whatever it is, their reactions are about them, not you.

The only person who can take responsibility for your happiness is you.

Sometimes you may find people in your circle being more active in their discouragement of your choices and the progress you are trying to make towards a happier life. Their reasons might be obvious and come from a good place: your mother doesn't want you to take a job overseas, your partner is worried that if you study at night you won't have time for him, or your best friend is worried that if you start a new relationship she will be alone on the dating circuit. In situations like this, the best you can do is reassure the other person of their significance in your life and hope they love and respect you enough not to try to undermine your decision.

If someone tries to undermine your commitment, re-evaluate your commitment to them.

Occasionally, you might find that someone you know actively tries to undermine you. The smoker who always offers you a cigarette, even though they know you are trying to quit. The 'friend' who serves cake although they know weight loss is your goal, or the colleague who undermines you in front of your boss. A true friend will support you on your path to success, regardless of their own goals, and a teammate plays for the whole team, not their personal agenda. If you find there are people in your life who are actively trying to undermine your commitment, perhaps you need to re-evaluate your commitment to them!

I remember when I was on my quest to bring more happiness into my life, one of the things I needed to do was what I call an *address book audit*. Some of my friends were actively supportive of the path I was on.

Others didn't understand the choices I was making but respected them all the same. But a few people, and fortunately it was only a few, actively sought to bring me down by constantly being negative about my choices and always trying to push their own fears and inadequacies onto me. I made the decision where possible to no longer mix with these people, or at the very least to limit my exposure to their toxicity.

It might seem like a tough decision, but if all your energy is going towards resisting their toxicity and sustaining your commitment when it feels like you are under fire, then it is really a matter of survival. It's important to remember that your commitment is *your* responsibility. Nobody can make you change your mind or get you to give up your chosen path. Only you can do that and as long as you choose not to, nobody else's opinion should get in your way. If you are going to be the best you can be, anyone who doesn't embrace or at the very least support you doesn't really belong in your world.

Tom Hanks, the star of *Forrest Gump* and many other award-winning films, says, 'If it wasn't hard, everyone would do it. It's the hard that makes it great'. Sadly, waiting for it to be easy is one of the main

reasons people don't make the changes they need
to make, to be truly happy and fulfilled in their life.
Very few *desired* changes can be achieved without
effort and a commitment to that effort. Whether the
change you want to make is logistical, like buying a
house or changing career, physical, like losing weight
or quitting smoking, or emotional, such as building
your confidence and developing your self-esteem, a
committed effort is always required. If you are not
consistent in your efforts and committed to those
efforts it will be much harder to get to where you
want to go. Rather than wait for things to be easy,
accept that while they may be challenging they will
definitely be worthwhile.

   If there are changes you want to make in your life,
take the time to think about why. Are you doing it
because it is expected of you, because somebody told
you to, or because you really and genuinely want to?
Sometimes the things that motivate you won't be the
obvious or expected drivers. I know this was the case
for me when in my mid-twenties I decided to quit
smoking. I wasn't a heavy smoker but I was definitely
addicted, needing my ciggie on the way to work, during
my coffee break, before lunch, after lunch and so on

at regular intervals throughout my day. Like most smokers I had quit before, twice, but as you know the key to stopping any bad habit is not starting again. Each time I had 'just one cigarette' I was sucked back into my smoking habit.

Very few changes in life are achieved without effort and a commitment to making that effort.

I knew smoking was bad for me, that it could kill me, but I figured I was young and I would stop smoking before the habit had the chance to do any lasting damage to my body. Just before my twenty-fourth birthday, I looked in the mirror and saw the first very fine lines on my forehead. I was mortified and saw this as being a big sign that my golden days of youth were coming to a close. This was all the motivation I needed to stop smoking. I realised the time had come to recognise that my body probably *was* beginning to be damaged by my habit. I would love to say that my health was my primary motivator, but in truth it was secondary. When I looked in the mirror and saw those fine lines on my face, I knew there was something I could do that would be better than any anti-ageing cream. I could stop smoking before any more signs of premature ageing appeared.

Identify your driving motivation and you will have all the encouragement you need.

I decided to stop smoking immediately. No hypnotism, no patches, no groups or other support. I just decided to never have another cigarette and that was over fifteen years ago. Was my real motivation vanity? Absolutely, but who cares as long as it helped me to make the change I needed to make.

Once you have identified your driving motivation you will have all the encouragement you need. Rather than waiting for things to become easy or forcing yourself into an uphill battle, harness the power of your motivation and rise to the challenge.

James knew all about challenges. He had been fighting a losing battle against his weight for the last ten years. Earlier in his life he had been very athletic, playing several sports at a competitive level until his mid-twenties, when a knee injury had put him on the bench. Somehow he had never found his way back onto the court. With each passing year he had put on more weight and although his knee had long recovered from the initial injury, carrying around a surplus fifty kilograms was putting his knee and every other joint in his body under strain.

James huffed and puffed at even the smallest physical exertion and he avoided it at all costs. James was caught in the vicious cycle of feeling bad about his weight and comforting himself with more food. His doctor had told him he needed to lose weight, his wife had begged him to do something about his health, but it wasn't until his son asked him why he couldn't kick the footy like the other dads that he was finally motivated to do something about it.

James had been attending his son's football grand final and after the match all the dads went out onto the pitch to kick the ball with their sons. He felt ashamed when his son asked him why he wasn't joining in and murmured something about his knee playing up. That night James looked in the mirror and promised himself he would become someone his son could be proud of. He vowed to lose the weight he needed to lose so that this time next year he too would be out there kicking the ball with his son.

James knew that fifty kilos was a lot of weight to lose so he went to his GP for advice. Given the strain his body was already under, his doctor advised against a drastic *Biggest Loser* quick fix and suggested that he instead adopt a diet and exercise plan he could sustain for life. The doctor also warned James that while some weight might 'fall off' in the beginning, it would be a long road and he should expect it to take a year or more to reach his goal weight.

When I met James, he was attending a conference at which I was speaking. We were talking about the power of setting goals and I had asked if anyone in the audience had any recent achievement they would like to share. The appearance of the tall, fit-looking man who stood up gave no indication of the journey he was about to share. James took the microphone and told the group of his weight-loss achievement. He explained how nothing had ever motivated him like the look of disappointment on his son's face and how his desire to be the kind of father his son could be proud of had fuelled his commitment on even the toughest days. When James finished his story there was barely a dry eye in the room. Not only had he shown the kind of commitment and determination his son could be truly proud of, but the other ninety-nine people in the room were feeling very proud for him too.

If you want to be the best you can be, the most important commitment you need to make is to becoming that person. Some of the changes you may need to make will be easier than others, but once you are committed to doing what it takes to have a happy and fulfilling life, becoming that person will be easy.

The most important commitment you will ever make is to being the best you can be.

The **Ninth Key** is all about the effort you are willing to make in order to have lasting happiness in your life. If you feel your commitment wavering, remind yourself that being the best you can be takes effort. Apply the *principle of commitment*; know that if you **keep it up** your efforts will be rewarded tenfold in the level of happiness and contentment in your life.

Be Brave

The Principle of Courage

Happiness begins with a choice, but it is your courage to pursue that choice that will determine if lifelong happiness and contentment are to be yours.

Being the best you can be takes courage. If you want to feel confident that you always do your best and know that your best was good enough, you need to commit to doing the right thing. This isn't just about moral decisions. Doing the right thing for *you* means deciding to do what most clearly reflects your sense of integrity, is consistent with your values and honours your beliefs.

So many people cruise through life taking the easy option. I'm not saying that to be the best you can be you should always take the hard road. Sometimes it will be easy, sometimes it will be tough and the majority of the time it will be somewhere in the middle. What matters is that you have the courage to own the decisions you need to make and are then brave enough to see them through once they have been made.

Being the best you can be takes courage. You need to own your decisions and have the courage to see them through.

Throughout life there will always be choices and decisions to make. Sometimes these will be about simple, day-to-day things, and other times about things that will have a more significant impact on your life. Occasionally an opportunity will arise that challenges you to do what really matters for yourself, for a loved one or for your community.

At times like this you may be tempted to 'hope for the best', 'turn a blind eye' or decide you 'don't want to get involved', but being the best you can be means doing what you know is right and not being complicit in your silence. Being the best you can be means that you are living your life with courageous integrity. This doesn't mean you have to go out and fight for a cause or begin a crusade, but you do need to make sure you can sleep at night confident in the knowledge that you have done the *right* thing, not the easy thing. As Oprah Winfrey explains, 'Real integrity is doing the right thing, knowing that nobody is going to know if you did it or not'.

Live your life with courageous integrity. Do the right thing, not the easy thing.

Society these days holds a much broader definition of what is right and wrong. Only a couple of generations ago it would have been shameful for a woman to have a child out of wedlock and yet these days few people would bat an eye. Where once it was considered immoral to have sex before you were married, many people now think it is wise to live with your partner before you marry, and while once upon a time a woman's place was in the home, the home is now just one of the many environments in which a woman can choose to excel.

In these modern times, we are largely free to choose our own moral code. You might think it's okay to watch movies that have been pirated as long as you have paid for them, or you might think this is just another form of theft. You may want to save yourself for the person you marry or instead enjoy a string of lovers. You might think a kiss is not being unfaithful, or you might think a single text is. Whatever your perspective, living your life with integrity means that once you are clear on your own moral position, you live by it. You will always be free to consciously change your mind or shift your perspective but you would never do something that you didn't believe in just because somebody else told you that you should.

Doing what other people think you should do is one of the biggest causes of unhappiness. Although this may be obvious when there are moral issues involved, for many people, doing what other people think they should be doing is less about acting without integrity and more about running out of energy.

Many are unhappy because they spend all of their time and energy keeping everyone else happy. They put all of their efforts into making sure everyone else is okay or avoiding the criticism of others. If you are constantly putting everyone else's needs ahead of yours, you can't expect to be happy. If you don't pay attention to your own needs or honour your values you will find yourself feeling resentful and compromised.

When I talk to clients about this, I often hear people say, 'But I don't want to be selfish'. The very nature of a selfish person ensures that being selfish is never one of their concerns. I find that most people, in their desire to avoid being selfish, are *selfless*. A selfless life is fine if you choose to join a convent or monastery, taking vows to abnegate your own needs and making your primary role one of worship and devotion. But if, like most people, you are actually trying to juggle a multitude of roles—wife, mother, boss, employee, employer, friend, relative and member of your community—and if you put all of the requirements of all of your roles ahead of yourself, there will be nothing left for you. And it's very hard to be happy if you are running on empty.

There is a big difference between being self-ist *and being selfish— putting yourself first doesn't mean you have to put everyone else last.*

There is a big difference between being selfish and being *self-ist.* People who are selfish do what they want, without caring what the consequences are for others. When you are *self-ist*, you attend to your needs and honour your values, while being respectful of those of others. You do the *right* thing for you, without doing the *wrong* thing by anyone else.

When I have this conversation with people who are parents, they often tell me that they have to put their children's needs first and to some extent I agree. If you are a parent, caring for your child *is* your most important role. But rarely is it your only role. I always suggest that my clients put the needs of the whole family first, rather than any one individual within it, but even if you believe that your children's needs should come first, that is still no excuse for putting yourself last.

It takes courage to honour your own needs and live in alignment with your values. It's actually much easier just to keep everyone else happy. That way nobody can be unhappy with you. When you start making your own needs a priority you may find some people in your life a little disgruntled. Why wouldn't they be? They're used to being put first in your life. It will take courage to explain that although they continue to be important to you, you have decided that you are important to you too.

Richard was the son of a very successful businessman and it was always assumed that when his father retired it would be up to him to take over his father's company. Richard had been groomed for this from a very young age and family dinners were spent discussing the comings and goings of the organisation. By the time Richard was eighteen, his life was mapped out for him.

He would go to a prestigious university in Australia and then on to an Ivy League business school in the US. Once he returned to Australia he would work in the family company, quickly moving up the ranks until his father felt confident his son could take over and he could retire.

Sometimes being happy will require some difficult conversations. Some of those conversations will be with yourself.

For a while everything went according to plan. That is, until Richard took on a senior role in the company and began to challenge the way his father did things. Times had changed since his father started the company and Richard was keen to take advantage of modern technology. He had also learned a lot about leadership while completing his MBA and he thought the company should move from his father's command-and-control regime to a management style that empowered employees.

Richard's father was not happy. He wanted *his* son to take over *his* business and run it the way *he* wanted it to be run. Richard felt very conflicted. When he first came to see me he thought the problem was the way he was communicating his ideas and perhaps he needed to change his approach. It soon became apparent that whatever approach Richard took the only one his father would accept was his own. The had a fundamental difference in both their values and their vision.

Richard knew he only had two options: to put up and shut up or to get out and go it alone. To complicate matters further, in one of their arguments, his father had made it quite clear that resigning was, in his opinion, not an option and threatened to 'cut him off' if he 'walked out'.

Richard felt torn. He was becoming more and more miserable working in his father's company, and the two men were at each other's throats nearly all of the time, but a future where his father had withdrawn not only his financial support, but also his emotional support, did not hold immediate appeal.

Richard felt moving to a competitor would be too disloyal and he started to think about going out on his own. While he wasn't enjoying working in his father's business, he liked the industry he was in and he was dying for the opportunity to put at least some of his ideas into action.

Richard knew the conversation with his father was going to be a difficult one. His father had been counting on him to take over the business since the day he was born and leaving now, with his father so close to retirement, would feel like the ultimate betrayal. But he also knew that for the sake of his sanity and his long-term relationship with his father it was something he was just going to have to do.

To be happy, you need to do the right thing for you, even when it feels like the hardest thing in the world.

It took a lot of courage for Richard to resign. His father was a powerful man and he had been raised to respect that power, but in putting his own needs first he had chosen to empower himself and begin his future as an independent man.

Making changes in your life takes courage but if you want to be free to be the best you can be you have to make the right decision, not the easy decision, even if it feels like the hardest thing in the world.

Richard was lucky; a combination of knowledge, experience and timing meant that his business was successful right from the very start. But not every change you make will be met with instant success. It is easy to be brave when everything is going well and all your plans are falling into place, but when the going gets tough it takes courage following the path you believe in.

If you want to be the best you can be you need to have the courage to be honest with yourself. This isn't a licence to pick yourself to pieces or engage in judgemental or self-critical behaviour. When you are honest with yourself, you are able to acknowledge all your positive qualities as well as those that don't serve you quite so well. When you know what is great about you, it is much easier to choose a course of action that will play to your strengths. When you know what areas have potential for improvement, you are able to make a concerted effort in a way that is sure to pay off.

It's easy to be brave when everything is going your way. When the going gets tough, it takes courage to follow the path you believe in.

Some people worry that being honest with themselves will make them unhappy. This is only the case if you have been living in denial. If you have been lying to yourself about the state of your body, your marriage, your career or any other aspect of your life, owning up to the truth can be confronting at first. But knowledge is power. Making the decision to be the best you can be will usually require making some changes, but if you are not honest with yourself about what those changes need to be, you won't know where to direct your efforts.

So many people tell themselves they are happy without stopping to question what that means. Rather than doing what they can to live their life in alignment with their values, they sweep any negative feelings or unsettling facts under the carpet. Instead of understanding what *real* success means to them, they fill their lives with the trappings of success and then wonder why the car, the house and the boat haven't made them happy.

Being the best you can be takes courage. It will always be easier to be average or a shadow of your potential. Gandhi said, 'The difference between what we do and what we are capable of doing would suffice to solve most of the world's problems'. Unless you are honest with yourself, you won't even be able to solve your own problems.

One of the hardest things for many people is simply saying 'no'. But what you say 'no' to in life will have just as much impact on your happiness as the things to which you say 'yes'. Some people say 'yes' to dinner invitations when they are really too tired to go, they say 'yes' to taking on more work when their day is already full and then say 'yes' to their children because they haven't got the energy to deal with the fuss that comes with saying 'no'.

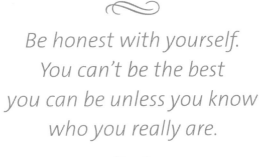

Be honest with yourself.
You can't be the best
you can be unless you know
who you really are.

They also lack the courage to say 'no' to some of the bigger things in life. Like turning down a promotion because in your heart you know you don't want the job; like walking away from temptation even if you've had a few too many drinks; or ending a relationship because it doesn't fulfil you or meet your needs.

When I decided it was time to change my life I had to say 'no' to my boss who was bullying me, and 'no' to the organisation that was enabling him. I had to say 'no' to a marriage proposal and 'no' when his sister told me it was the mistake of my life, and, years later, I said 'no' to the big bucks because I knew I wanted a different life. Unless you have the courage to say 'no' to the things you don't want, it is hard to be brave enough to say 'yes' to all that you do want.

Unless you have the courage to say 'no' to the things you don't want, it's hard to say 'yes' to the things that you do want.

Tara started her career as a model. She had a beautiful face and a ready smile, and was a natural in front of the camera. She quickly progressed from doing television commercials to being the 'sidekick' on a popular TV show. When Tara came to see me she was at a crossroads. The previous year she had acted in a short film and much to her surprise her performance had won critical acclaim. Being in the television industry, Tara had toyed with the idea of acting, but was always put off by the 'model-turned-actress' tag. She loved presenting but the idea of being someone else had never really appealed. In fact, the only reason she had taken the part in the film in the first place was as a favour to the director, who was a friend.

Now everyone was saying she had potential. Her agent wanted her to work with an acting coach and was pressing her to think about 'pilot season' in LA. At the same time this sudden buzz around her meant that offers were flowing in for presenting work too. The offer that most appealed to Tara was the chance to be part of a new format for a celebrity entertainment show. It wasn't *Dancing with the Stars* or *Dancing on Ice*, but there was definitely going to be dancing and Tara thought it sounded brilliant.

Unfortunately, the offer that appealed most to Tara was the one her agent was most strenuously advising her against. He felt that the recognition of her recent performance combined with her golden girl looks meant she was ready for the next big step in her career. Her acting career. He said he was certain if she went on the celebrity dance show she would lose all the credibility she had recently earned as an actor and her career would be over before it begun.

Tara didn't know what to do. I told her I thought it was important to put aside the recent hype and get back to basics. What were her values, what motivated her at work and what did she want her future to look like? Tara had been so busy weighing up what everyone said she should do that she hadn't stopped to think about what she wanted to do.

As soon as Tara was honest with herself her answer became clear. She realised that although many of the opportunities that were coming in were good offers, it didn't automatically mean that they were right for her, and while a lot of her colleagues in the industry would kill to be in her shoes they were never shoes she particularly wanted to wear.

Knowing what you don't want is just as important as knowing what you do want, and it is only when you are really honest with yourself that these answers can come to light. You need to be brave enough to walk away from what other people say you should be doing and have the courage to do what is right for you.

Don't rely on the opinions of others. Only you will know what is right for you.

Tara didn't want to be an actress. She loved being in front of the camera, but she didn't want to have to repeat the same line over and over again and she couldn't bear the thought of learning to be somebody else. Tara realised she loved being on *live* camera, where her adrenalin was pumping and her true personality had the chance to shine through. She wasn't afraid of a challenge, but she wanted work to be filled with fun and laughter, not learning to cry on cue. Her agent said it was a risky decision, but Tara knew accepting the dancing show was the right thing for her.

Tara had chosen to engage the services of her agent so it was right that she considered his view. The majority of the time when people tell you what they think, they are telling you what would be right for them. But unless you have actively solicited an opinion, you are under no obligation to consider it, let alone accept it.

If you want to be the best you can be you need to have the courage to be your own counsel. Although you may occasionally seek the opinions of others, you know the only one who knows the right answer for *you* is you.

Being the best you can be means living fearlessly. This doesn't mean being foolish or making reckless decisions. When you are courageous in your decision-making, you are honest with yourself about all the risks and potential consequences. You consider your values and priorities and know that once you have made up your mind, regardless of what the future holds, you will never look back.

Be courageous in your decision-making. Stand by your choices and never look back.

The **Tenth Key** is all about finding the courage to be the best you can be. Next time you find yourself worrying about what people might think or say about the choices you are making, remind yourself that fortune favours the bold. Apply the *principle of courage*; **be brave** and know that your life is guaranteed to be rich in every way.

Unlocking the Code
Applying the Ten Keys to Your Life

I hope you have found *The Happiness Code* to be an exciting and inspiring discovery. Perhaps on some level knowing that enduring happiness will be the result of not the things you've done, but the person you've chosen to be, will be a relief. I know it was for me. Don't let this book get dusty. Keep it close by and know that whenever you don't feel as happy as you could, the solution lies within one of the **Ten Keys**.

If you would like to learn more about *The Happiness Code* and how to apply the **Ten Keys** to your life, visit **domoniquebertolucci.com**. Don't forget to download and work through *The Happiness Code Workbook* if you haven't already done so and let me know what impact applying the **Ten Keys** has had on your life at **facebook.com/domoniquebertolucci**.

Finishing this book is really just the beginning. You now hold the keys to lifelong happiness and contentment. The best way to think of the **Ten Keys** is as guiding principles for a life where you:

- make strong conscious choices
- recognise the things you have control over and let go of all that you don't
- live in the moment and enjoy each day for what it is
- expect the best from life
- believe in yourself, in your dreams and in your right to pursue those dreams
- give yourself permission to do, be and have all that you can in life
- remember, despite all you may still want, to feel gratitude for how rich your life already is
- are generous, not just with your money, but with your spirit, your time and your energy, and don't judge
- commit to being the best you can be
- find the courage to become that person.

When you live your life by these principles, you can release yourself from the burden of perfectionism, let go of your frustrations and anxieties and relax, confident in the knowledge you are being *the best you can be*.

Acknowledgements

My first thanks go to my wonderful agent Tara Wynne at Curtis Brown for her unwavering belief in my work, and to Sharon Mullins, my commissioning editor at Hardie Grant, for making *The Happiness Code* a reality.

Thank you to Fiona Hardie, Sandy Grant, Allison Hiew, Brooke Clark, Raylee Sloane, Rosalind McClintock and the rest of the team at Hardie Grant for being such a pleasure to work with.

To my dear friend, Brooke Alexander, thank you for being the first person I speak to about each and every idea I have for my business—our conversations always leave me feeling inspired and excited about the world I am working to create.

Although some of the details have been changed (for privacy), the stories in this book are all based on my work. Thank you to each of my clients past and present, as well as to all of the inspiring people who have attended my workshops, for inviting me to share your journey with you. Working with you is both an honour and a privilege and I am humbled to have learned so much from you.

Thank you to Mum and Dad, my brother Jeff, and Nonna and Auntie Laurel for being the founding members of my fan club. Your unconditional love and support means everything to me. Thank you, too, to my extended family, including the Willises and the Peterkins, for being so enthusiastic about each of my endeavours.

To my darling Sophia, thank you for being an endless source of joy in my life, and to Paul, for everything, always.

About the
Author

Domonique Bertolucci is the closely guarded secret
behind some of the country's most successful people.

Passionate about *real success*, she has a client list that
reads like a who's who of CEOs and corporate figures,
award-winning entrepreneurs and celebrities, and her
workshops are attended by people from all walks of life,
from all around the world. A regular on the corporate
speaking circuit, Domonique challenges her audience
to think about what it is they really want from life, and
why they haven't been living that way up until now.

Born in Australia, Domonique's first career as a
fashion model took her to London at twenty-two
where, realising she was never going to be a 'waif', she
underwent a different type of extreme makeover: from
model to corporate high-flyer. After ten years in the
cutthroat world of investment banking she returned to
Australia and established her coaching practice.

Since writing her first book, *Your Best Life*, in 2006, Domonique has become Australia's most popular life coach. More than ten million people have seen, read or heard her advice.

Domonique divides her time between Sydney and London. She lives with her husband and young daughter and in her spare time can be found with her nose in a book, watching a movie, practising yoga or keeping up the great Italian tradition of feeding the people that you love.

domoniquebertolucci.com

facebook.com/domoniquebertolucci

twitter.com/fromDomonique